W9-CKT-006

One Church Many Cultures

Challenge of Diversity

Joseph P. Fitzpatrick, S.J.

Sheed & Ward

Scripture references are taken from **The Jerusalem Bible**.

Copyright © 1987
Joseph P. Fitzpatrick

All rights reserved. No part of this book may be
reproduced or transmitted in any form or by any
means, electronic or mechanical, including photo-
copying, recording or by an information storage
and retrieval system without permission in writing
from the Publisher.

Sheed & Ward™ is a service of National Catholic
Reporter Publishing, Inc.

Library of Congress Catalog Card Number: 86-61359

ISBN: 0-934134-63-4

Published by: Sheed & Ward
115 E. Armour Blvd. P.O. Box 414292
Kansas City, MO 64141-0281

To order, call: (800) 821-7926

Contents

Preface   1

1. The Church as Catholic: One Faith with Many
   Cultural Manifestations   7

2. Culture   27

3. Some Historic Adaptations of the Faith
   to Cultures   53

4. The American Experience   95

5. Hispanics in the United States   125

6. Religion and Culture: Theological
   Reflections   167

PREFACE

In the 1974 Synod of Bishops, convoked by Pope Paul VI, the impact of the bishops from the Third World was emphatic.[1] It was another significant moment when the Church realized that its future may well emerge in the developing nations. For this to happen, the miracle of the Church must occur again — the continuing unity of the church in the presence of decidedly different cultures. As the Church in its early days was able to break out of the limitations of the religious tradition of the Hebrews and find its fulfillment in Greek and Roman ways of life, so again it faces the challenge of breaking out of the limitations of Western Christianity to find its fulfillment in Asian and African ways of life.

The bishops saw clearly in their midst the variety of the Church's life and the fulfillment of the prayer of Jesus "that they all may be one." They also realized that if this unity and diversity were to go forward in the modern world, it would not be able to do so within a Western style of life. Fortunately this is not a new challenge. It began with the request of the first gentile for baptism, when the apostles faced the problem of the relationship of Jewish Christians to a gentile world. It has continued through a turbulent history to the present day. It prompted the impressive statement on "The Church and Culture"[2] in the *Constitution on the Church in the Modern World* in Vatican II. This document has been followed by numerous conferences, declarations, and publications about the relationship of the Church to the variety of cultures in today's world, especially the non-Christian cultures.

The Synod of Bishops of 1974 addressed itself directly to the issue of evangelization, the task of bringing the message of the Gospel to non-Christian people. This was followed by the Apostolic Exhortation of Paul VI, *The Evangelization of Peoples*.[3]

More recently, Pope John Paul II issued an Encyclical,

1

Slavorum Apostoli[4] commemorating the work of two apostles, Saints Cyril and Methodius, who achieved one of the greatest adaptations of Catholic beliefs and practices to the new and strange population of Slavic people. Its theme is the challenge of maintaining the unity of the church in the presence of different cultures.

These documents will be examined in detail later. They provide an ideal point of reference for the present book, which seeks to take advantage of the social sciences to clarify the nature of the challenge and the ways in which the Church has sought to respond to it.

More than ever before, the Catholic Church faces the challenge of responding to the vast variety of ways of life throughout the world, "cultures" as they are called in the sociological and theological discussions of the issue. How is the Church going to bring the life and teaching of Jesus in a meaningful way to people who think in ways very different from that of Western Europeans, and whose lives are penetrated totally with religious beliefs and practices very different from those of the Christian lands of the West; to people who now constitute the great majority of humankind? That is only one challenge. It is clearly recognized now that many of the lands that call themselves Christian are suffering a loss of faith and are characterized by social institutions that perpetuate injustice and oppression, and that the so-called developed world has been dominated by a secularism that has been harmful to the continuing influence of Christianity.

This statement of challenges seems to be too negative. The remarkable *Constitution of the Church in the Modern World (Gaudium et Spes)*, of the Second Vatican Council, sees a positive and promising hope in the challenge, a world of new ideas, new insights into the nature of humankind and the world, and a potential for the growth of the Church that has not existed before. Central to the challenge and the response is the question of culture: how the life and word of Jesus is to be given expression in cultures that are so different from or opposed to it.

There are two dimensions to the issue. The first one is practical: how has the Church met this challenge in the past; how is it preparing to meet the challenge at the present? Some of the significant moments in this history will be examined in this book. Chapter 4 will give a brief history of the Slavonic Rites and the Chinese Rites, both extraordinary adaptations of the Catholic faith to new and strange cultures; the first was approved, the second was condemned.

As for the present, conferences are convened, training programs conducted, cultures are carefully studied, and theological reflection is pursued as religious persons seek to prepare themselves for the practical task of bringing the Gospel to others. Institutions like the Institute of Intercultural Communication, which existed in Ponce, Puerto Rico, from 1957-72, or the Mexican American Cultural Center (MACC), now flourishing in San Antonio, Texas, are two examples of efforts in the United States to prepare Catholics to meet the challenge. The East Asia Pastoral Institute is a regional center of study and policy on the international scene.

These have been training centers where the study of language and culture enable Catholics to communicate with persons of differing cultures and to understand the way of life of the people to whom they are ministering. More will be said about them later.

There is also a second dimension, theological particularly, but involving the social sciences, which seeks to deal with the more fundamental issue: what is essential to the Catholic faith; what are the cultural characteristics in which the Faith can be given adequate expression; what are the cultural characteristics that are not compatible? From the first revelation to Saint Peter on the rooftop at Joppa (Acts 10) and the First Council of Jerusalem (Acts 15) to the present, this has been a recurring problem for the church. By reflecting on some of the experiences of the past, we may be able to prepare ourselves for the challenge of the present.

This book, then, is a brief overview of the question, designed for the intelligent and concerned religious persons who may have to prepare for a ministry to persons of different language and cultural background from themselves; and for intelligent and concerned readers who may wish to understand a little more clearly the nature of this current challenge the Church is facing. It is not a theological treatise, although the last chapter seeks to present a brief review of the theological discussions that are taking place. Nor is it a practical handbook, a how-to-do-it resource, to give people practical guidance. It is designed to provide some insight into the problem for ordinary Christians to help them appreciate the promise and the problem of the increasing contact of the Faith with the cultures of the modern world.

Perhaps a word about myself would be helpful. I was first introduced to the problem of intercultural differences and intercultural understanding and communication in graduate classes at Harvard University with Professor Talcott Parsons, at that time one of the most influential sociologists in the United States. His lectures on "Comparative Institutions" opened my eyes and my mind to worlds of which I was unaware. My first paper for the course was a study of Matteo Ricci, the great Jesuit who developed the Chinese Rites. The study was not only an important religious experience for me; it was an interesting revelation to many of my professors and fellow students who were unaware of that remarkable history. Other courses on "Boston's Immigrants" with Professor Oscar Handlin, the well-known historian of American immigration, made me aware for the first time of what it means to be Irish. His explanations of the clash of cultures between the Irish and the Boston Protestants not only filled me in on my own people and my Irish background; they prepared me for the experience I was to face in New York City.

I began a career as a sociology professor at Fordham University in 1949, just as the Puerto Rican migration was increasing. It was the background at Harvard that enabled me to perceive the problems, both for Puerto Ricans and for New Yorkers, in the arrival of hundreds of thousands of newcomers from Puerto

Rico. I found myself called upon repeatedly to help others, in social agencies, in schools and police precincts, in hospitals and parishes, to understand the background of the Puerto Rican people and their problems of adjustment to New York. Conferences and workshops on intercultural understanding and communication became a dominant feature of my life. I became involved in the efforts of the Church to prepare to respond to the Puerto Rican presence. I participated with Monsignor Ivan Illich in the development of the Institute of Intercultural Documentation at the Catholic University of Puerto Rico in Ponce, Puerto Rico, where hundreds of priests, Sisters, Brothers, and lay persons prepared themselves for ministry to Puerto Ricans either in Puerto Rico or on the mainland. Later I collaborated with Ivan Illich in the establishment of the Center of Intercultural Documentation at Cuernavaca, Mexico, where the larger issues of the Church and the cultures of the world became topics of daily discussions. In all of these experiences, I was aware of the strong desire of so many persons to understand, to appreciate, and to be able to relate with understanding and sympathy (in the true Spanish meaning of *simpatico*) with persons of different cultures. At Fordham University I developed courses in Cultural Assimilation and Comparative Cultures, as well as more theoretical studies of the relationship of faith, theology, and the humanities to the social sciences. I have often wanted to write down, however, briefly, some of the results of this long experience, to assist persons like the many students I was privileged to teach. The present book is an attempt to do this, an attempt to help others gain some of the insight I have found helpful myself; to understand a little better the challenge to the Church in its relation to the cultures of the world; to recognize this as a gift from the Lord at the present time; and to appreciate the rich increase of life that awaits the Church and the cultures with which she comes in contact, as they come to share with each other the blessings of their particular ways of life.

In the preparation of this book I am indebted to the Loyola Foundation for a helpful research grant. I am indebted to hundreds of others, from University professors with their ideas to humble peasants of Mexico and Puerto Rico who have revealed to me how faith gives profound meaning to their lives. Two persons I must mention by name: Ivan Illich, who opened the minds and hearts of thousands of my generation and gave us a vision of extraordinary importance at a critical moment of the Church's life; and the late Dorothy M. Dohen, whose remarkable perception of faith and culture provided a realistic balance to the visions of Ivan Illich. Finally, a word of thanks to my secretary, Paula Genova, whose competence and patience keep a reasonable amount of order in my life and work.

Notes

1. The Declaration of the Synod, *Evangelization of the Modern World*, is found in Joseph Gremillion (ed.), *The Gospel of Peace and Justice* (Maryknoll, New York: Orbis Press, 1976), pp. 593-98.

2. *The Pastoral Constitution on the Church in the Modern World (Gaudium et Spes)* Part 2, Chapter 2, "The Proper Development of Culture," in Walter M. Abbott, S.J. (ed.), *The Documents of Vatican II* (New York: Herder and Herder, 1966).

3. Pope Paul VI, *Evangelization in the Modern World (Evangelii Nuntiandi)* Apostolic Exhortation of Pope Paul VI, (Dec. 8, 1975) AAS, LXVIII (1/31/76), pp. 5-76. English translation is published in *The Pope Speaks*, V. 21, n. 1 (1976), pp. 4-51.

4. Pope John Paul II, Encyclical: *Slavorum Apostoli*, June 2, 1985. In *Origins*, V. 15, n. 8 (July 18, 1985).

1
THE CHURCH
AS CATHOLIC:[1] ONE FAITH
WITH MANY CULTURAL
MANIFESTATIONS

The life and word of Jesus were one; but His final mandate to the apostles was, "Go and make disciples of all nations." This would bring the Gospel into contact with a multiplicity of languages, life styles, and ways of thinking and believing; in brief, what anthropologists today call "cultures." By making "disciples of all nations," did Jesus mean to homogenize the world and eliminate the cultural varieties of the human family? Or was the Gospel to be accepted and fulfilled in a variety of ways, within the context of a multiplicity of cultures? Unity in multiplicity: but in what way? One Kingdom of the Lord, but with many mansions: how would this occur? I pray, Father: "May they all be one. Father may they be one in us as you are in me and I in you . . . may they be so completely one that the world will realize it was you who sent me" (John 17:21-23). But was the unity in faith to be a similarity of cultures? Or was it to be a unity that was "Catholic," one faith capable of manifesting itself in the context of a variety of cultures? How would this take place?

This is the problem of the faith and cultures. In this book, the focus is on the relationship of the Catholic faith to the variety of cultures among the nations which were to become disciples of Jesus. This critical issue first appeared when Cornelius, a Roman officer in Palestine, asked for baptism (Acts 10). Until he sought to become a Christian, all the followers of Jesus had

7

been Jews, circumcised under the Law of Moses and observing the precepts of the law in the tradition of the Hebrews. But with Cornelius, here was an uncircumcised Gentile, living in a Roman culture, seeking to become a disciple of the Lord and asking for baptism. What were the apostles to do? Were they to require that he become circumcised and follow the Mosaic Law, in brief, accept the Hebrew culture and way of life? Or was he to remain a Gentile and a Roman, as he became a Christian? God settled the issue in a revelation to Peter. "What God has made clean, you have no right to call profane." And Peter explained the revelation to the family of Cornelius: "The truth that I have now come to realize is that God does not have favorites, but that anybody of any nationality who fears God and does what is right is acceptable to Him." Cornelius was to remain a Roman; he would not be circumcised and required to live as the Hebrews lived. He would be a disciple of Jesus within the context of a Roman culture and way of life. The one Faith and Gospel of Jesus would fulfill itself in a multiplicity of cultures. It sounded easy.

However, this was not the end, but the beginning of problems. The relationship of the Faith to the variety of cultures was to prove one of the most difficult and troublesome features of the Church's life, from the days of the apostles down to the present. It was the issue that led to the First Council of the Church at Jerusalem (Acts 15). Were the Gentile Christians to be required to observe any provisions of the Mosaic Law? The decision was "no." It was again a major issue at the Second Vatican Council, and it resulted in the remarkable statement on the Church and cultures in the *Pastoral Constitution of the Church in the Modern World*. The principles have always been clear; it is in the practice that the difficulties emerge.

The problem arises in three situations: first, when Christians (or Catholics) seek to bring the Faith to people of a culture other than their own, they face the problem of determining how the Faith is to express itself in this different way of life. This is the problem of "inculturation." Secondly, when Christians (Catholics) of a particular cultural background migrate to an area of different language and culture, to what extent may they continue practicing the faith in their own cultural style, or must they modify their beliefs and practices to conform to the culture of the area to which they have come? This is the problem of cultural integration or cultural pluralism. The bishops of the United States, for example, in their Pastoral Letter, *The Hispanic Presence: Challenge and Commitment*,[2] have asked for a policy of cultural pluralism, a situation in which Hispanic newcomers can feel confident and free to continue to practice their faith in their traditional way while at the same time they have the confidence that they are completely welcome among those who practice the faith in a more American style. The practical pastoral problems involved in this are very serious. They are simply examples of the continuing presence of this abiding problem in the life of the Church.

Thirdly, a relatively new but equally challenging problem has arisen in recent years: the recognition that justice is an essential component of faith. This insight developed out of the realization that, among many peoples calling themselves Christian, social institutions are marked by injustice, exploitation, and violent oppression of the poor. Consequently, if faith is to express itself within these cultures, this "inculturation" will involve the Christian commitment to justice and the liberation of the poor.

The present book is an effort to look at this problem in a contemporary perspective: to examine it with the help of some concepts from the social sciences; to describe some historical examples of the response of the Church to experiments in cultural adaptation of the Faith; to review the experience of the Church in the United States; and to try to give some guidance to the Church, its leaders and members as they face the practical issues of the Faith and culture in their own lives.

This first chapter will review the emergence of the problem in the early days of the Church and the official response of the apostles as the leaders of the Church in those days. The second chapter will explain culture as this concept and term have been developed in the social sciences. It is a concept which has given extraordinary insight into the nature of the social behavior of men and women. When analyzed in the context of the concept of culture, the relation of the Faith to the variety of life styles of Christians (Catholics) becomes much clearer. In view of this it helps to perceive the problem as a problem of "communication" as social scientists understand it, namely the ability to perceive the meaning of the behavior of others and the ability to communicate to these others the meaning that things have for me. This will be analyzed in detail in Chapter 2.

With this background, some of the historical experiments in the adaptation of the faith to cultures will be described and the American experience in particular will be analyzed, especially in view of the present influx of Hispanics. Finally, in the context of all these aspects of the study, an attempt will be made to state briefly but clearly the various positions currently being presented by theologians, religious leaders, and authorities in the Church about the question of faith and culture.

It is, as will be seen, a complicated and difficult issue. This book will not provide a solution to the problem. Perhaps it will provide some insight that may help the reader to understand the problem, and give some guidance to those who must face the problem in their pastoral work or their theological reflection.

The Emerging Crisis: The Conversion of Cornelius

The problem of faith in Jesus and its relation to a multiplicity of cultures burst upon the early Church suddenly and unexpectedly. It was the occasion of a divine intervention — before the fact, one of the clearest and most striking revelations in the history of the Church, guiding it in its relationship to the Gentile world. As indicated above, all the early followers of Jesus were Jews, devoutly following the Mosaic Law, the Hebrew way of life. Suddenly an uncircumcised Gentile, an officer of the Roman army of occupation in Palestine, asked for baptism. This raised the critical issue: were they to insist that Cornelius be circumcised, accept the Mosaic Law, and live according to its precepts? In brief, was Cornelius to be required to follow the Hebrew way of life in order to become a Christian? The history is given in Acts 10, a remarkable account of the opening of the Church to the Gentile world. Without the specific details of the narrative in Acts, it would be difficult to appreciate the meaning of the event. Thus they will be presented at some length in the following pages.

The revelation to guide the Church was given to Peter, another indication of the primary role he played among the apostles. It is important here to quote the history of the event.

Acts X

Peter Visits a Roman Centurion

One of the centurions of the Italica cohort stationed in Caesarea was called Cornelius. He and the whole of his household were devout and God-fearing, and he gave generously to Jewish causes and prayed constantly to God.

One day at about the ninth hour he had a vision in which he distinctly saw the angel of God come into his house and call out to him, "Cornelius!" He stared at the vision in terror and exclaimed, "What is it, Lord?" "Your offering of prayers and alms," the angel answered, "has been accepted by God. Now you must send someone to Jaffa and fetch a man called Simon, known as Peter, who is lodging with Simon the tanner whose house is by the sea." When the angel who said this had gone, Cornelius called two of the slaves and a devout soldier of his staff, told them what happened, and sent them off to Jaffa.

Next day, while they were still on their journey and had only a short distance to go before reaching Jaffa, Peter went to the housetop at about the sixth hour to pray. He felt hungry and was looking forward to his meal, but before it was ready he fell into a trance and saw heaven thrown open and something like a big sheet being let down to earth by its four corners; it contained every possible sort of animal and bird, walking, crawling or flying ones. A voice then said to him, "Now, Peter; kill and eat!" But Peter answered, "Certainly not, Lord; I have never yet eaten anything profane or unclean." Again, a second time, the voice spoke to him, "What God has made clean, you have no right to call profane." This was repeated three times, and then suddenly the container was drawn up to heaven again.

Peter was still worrying over the meaning of the vision he had seen, when the men sent by Cornelius arrived. They had asked where Simon's house was and they were now standing at the door, calling out to know if the Simon known as Peter was lodging there. Peter's mind was still on the vision and the Spirit had to tell him, "Some men have come to see you. Hurry down, and do not hesitate about going back with them; it was I who told them to come." Peter went down and said to them, "I am the man you are looking for; why have you come?" They said, "The centurion Cornelius, who is an upright and God-fearing man, highly regarded by the entire Jewish people, was directed by a holy angel to send for you and bring you to his house and to listen to what you have to say." So Peter asked them in and gave them lodging.

Next day, he was ready to go off with them, accompanied by some of the brothers from Jaffa. They reached Caesarea the following day, and Cornelius was waiting for them. He had asked his relations and close friends to be there and as Peter reached the house Cornelius went out to meet him, knelt at his feet and prostrated himself. But Peter helped him up. "Stand up," he said, "I am only a man after all!" Talking together they went in to meet all the people assembled there, and Peter said to them, "You know it is forbidden for Jews to mix with people of another race and visit them, but God has made it clear to me that I must not call anyone profane or unclean. That is why I made no objection to coming when I was sent for; but I should like to know exactly why you sent for me."

Cornelius replied, "Three days ago I was praying in my house at the ninth hour, when I suddenly saw a man in front of me in shining robes. He said, 'Cornelius, your prayer has been heard and your alms have been accepted as a sacrifice in the sight of God; so now you must send to Jaffa and fetch Simon known as Peter who is lodging in the house of Simon the tanner, by the sea.' So I sent for you at once, and you have been kind enough to come. Here we all are, assembled in front of you to hear what message God has given you for us."

Peter's Address in the House of Cornelius

Then Peter addressed them: "The truth I have now come to realize," he said, "is that God does not have favorites, but that anybody of any nationality who fears God and does what is right is acceptable to him.

"It is true, God sent his word to the people of Israel, and it was to them that *the good news of peace was brought* by Jesus Christ — but Jesus Christ is Lord of all men. You must have heard about the recent happenings in Judaea; about Jesus of Nazareth and how he began in Galilee, after John had been preaching baptism. *God had anointed him with the Holy Spirit* and with power, and because God was with him, Jesus went about doing good and curing all who had fallen into the power of the devil. Now I, and those with me, can witness to everything he did throughout the countryside of Judaea and in Jerusalem itself: and also to the fact that they killed him by hanging him on a tree, yet three days afterwards God raised him to life and allowed him to be seen, not by the whole people but only by certain witnesses God had chosen beforehand. Now we are those witnesses — we have eaten and drunk with him after his resurrection from the dead — and he has ordered us to proclaim this to his people and to tell them that God has appointed him to judge everyone, alive or dead. It is to him that all the prophets bear this witness: that all who believe in Jesus will have their sins forgiven through his name."

Baptism of the First Pagans

While Peter was still speaking the Holy Spirit came down on all the listeners. Jewish believers who had accompanied Peter were all astonished that the gift of the Holy Spirit should be poured out on the pagans too, since they could hear them speaking strange languages and proclaiming the greatness of God. Peter himself then said, "Could anyone refuse the water of baptism to these people, now they have received the Holy Spirit just as much as we have?" He then gave orders for them to baptized in the name of Jesus Christ. Afterwards they begged him to stay on for some days.

The Mosaic Law, The Hebrew Way of Life

To understand the problem involved in the conversion of Cornelius, it is necessary to understand something of the history and tradition of the Hebrew people. They were chosen by God as His own People; God struck a covenant between Himself and them, sealed in the blood that Moses sprinkled on the people and on the altar. In the book of Exodus (10 ff.) many of the laws are given about the life and worship of the Hebrews. Then follows the book of Leviticus, with all the details of the law to be followed. These were part of the covenant struck between God and His People. If they were faithful to Him, God promised the Hebrews a land of their own, flowing with milk and honey.

The Mosaic Law as a Culture

When the precepts of the Law are analyzed, they constitute what modern anthropologists would call a culture: relations between husbands and wives, even to the most intimate details such as when they could have intercourse; relations between masters and slaves, parents and children. The Law governed the relationships of Jews to Gentiles; when Jews could work; what they could eat and how it must be prepared; when they could take a journey. There was not a segment of human behavior that it did not touch upon and regulate. Briefly, God identified His revelation to the Hebrews with a culture.

The study of primitive peoples gives some suggestions as to why God should have done this. Historically, at the early stages of cultural development, expressions of religious belief tend to become rigidly associated with particular forms of behavior. Fidelity to a people's gods tends to be expressed in strict adherence to ritualistic practices. Exact punishment is visited upon a person for specific violations of the law.

For the Hebrews, the Law was rooted in the covenant by which they were named as the chosen people of the Lord. If they were faithful to Him, He would be faithful to them. The Law, therefore, became the great tradition of the Hebrew people. It was a burdensome discipline, as Paul so frequently states in his letters. And it was abused in the casuistry of the religious leaders of the Jewish people. The severe imprecations of Jesus against the Scribes and Pharisees were prompted by the rigid interpretation of the Law, a rigidity, as Jesus complained, in which the spirit of the Law was smothered in the overemphasis on external ritual observance.

Nevertheless, the Law was the link between themselves and God, and devout Jews made every effort to be faithful to it. They suffered and sacrificed to observe it. On many occasions they accepted persecution or death rather than deviate from it. The history of the Maccabees is only one of many examples of the heroism associated with its observance. Fidelity to this tradition was the mark of the loyal member of the Lord's People. The reversal in favor of the Gentiles was terribly difficult for the Jewish Christians to understand. The Law was the great sign and symbol of the bond between God and His people. And here was Peter telling them that it did not mean anything anymore. They had no way of conceiving how God's people could be united with Him and manifest their fidelity to Him except through the observance of the Law. And now Peter was teaching that God revealed to him that the Gentiles were to be as acceptable to God as the Jews!

Yet this was precisely the fulfillment of God's gift to all His people, as Peter stated it in the home of Cornelius. "Could anyone refuse water for these to be baptized, seeing that they have received the Spirit the same way we have?" Paul stated it in more detail and more powerfully in his letter to the Ephesians (3:1-21).

> So I, Paul, a prisoner of Christ Jesus for the sake of you pagans. . . . You have probably heard how I have been entrusted by God with the grace he meant for you, and that it was by a revelation that I was given the knowledge of the mystery, as I have just described it very shortly. If you read my words, you will have some idea of the depths that I see in the mystery of Christ. This mystery that has now been revealed through the Spirit to this holy apostles and prophets was unknown to any men in past generations, it means that pagans now share the same inheritance, that they are parts of the same body, and that the same promise has been made to them, in Christ Jesus, through the gospel. I have been made the servant of that gospel by a gift of grace from God who gave it to me by his own power. I, who am less than the least of all saints, have been entrusted with this special grace, not only of proclaiming to the pagans the infinite treasure of Christ but also of explaining how the mystery is to be dispensed. Through all the

ages, this has been kept hidden in God, the creator of everything. Why? So that the Sovereignties and Powers should learn only now, through the Church, how comprehensive God's wisdom really is, exactly according to the plan which he had had from all eternity in Christ Jesus our Lord. This is why we are bold enough to approach God in complete confidence, through our faith in him; so, I beg you, never lose confidence just because of the trials that I go through on your account: they are your glory.

Paul's prayer

This, then, is what I pray, kneeling before the Father, from whom every family, whether spiritual or natural, takes its name:

"Out of his infinite glory, may he give you the power through his Spirit for your hidden self to grow strong, so that Christ may live in your hearts through faith, and then, planted in love and built on love, you will with all the saints have strength to grasp the breadth and the length, the height and the depth; until, knowing the love of Christ which is beyond all knowledge, you are filled with the utter fullness of God.

"Glory be to him whose power, working in us, can do infinitely more than we can ask or imagine; glory be to him from generation to generation in the Church and in Christ Jesus for ever and ever. Amen."

This is the great statement by Paul of his vision of the infinite wisdom and goodness of God, namely, God's plan to give to all men and women a share in the life of Jesus, the fulfillment of the promises of the Law. All nations in Christ were to be the people of God, the chosen ones, destined for the same eternal destiny as had been originally promised to the Jews. The significance of the revelation to Peter was the fact that the Mosaic Law was no longer to be the bond between God and His people. A new covenant had been struck in the blood of Jesus; a new testament established with all who would believe in Him and live according to His law of love, which replaced the strict discipline of the Law as given to Moses. "By this shall all know you are my disciples that you love one another" (John 13:35).

The Growing Conflict[3]

The great revelation had been given to Peter. It was actually to be fulfilled by the preaching of Paul. The place where the conflict erupted seriously was in Antioch. Antioch was the city where the first large Gentile community of Christians developed. The apostles were not prepared to evangelize the pagan world. They spoke no Greek, a common language in those days. They had no familiarity with the style of life of the non-Jewish world. When word came of the growth of the Church in Antioch, the apostles sent Barnabas to minister to it. Barnabas had come from Cyprus; he knew Greek and was familiar with the non-Jewish world. Barnabas remembered Saul, who had withdrawn to Tarsus, his native city, some years previously when it was clear it was not safe for him to be around Jerusalem. Barnabas called Saul (now Paul) to Antioch. Under the care of Barnabas and Paul, the Gentile community at Antioch began to flourish.

Antioch was a political and commercial crossroads in the middle east.[4] It was a center where Syrians, Romans, Greeks, Egyptians, and many other nationalities met in pursuit of trade. It was chosen by the Romans as the administrative center of the occupation forces of the near East. The Roman engineers rerouted the river that twisted its way through the city, cascading the river down the main avenue and setting up torches on each side that were lighted at night. It was a center of athletic games, dramatic performances, circuses, and entertainment. It was a city also of intense political activity and intrigue. It was out of this mixed group of men and women that the first Gentile church came into being.

Paul was the great champion of the freedom of the Gentiles from the bonds of the Mosaic Law. He insisted that he also had received this from Jesus in a revelation that taught him the life and way of Jesus. In Galatians 1 he describes his conversion and the revelation he received on that occasion. Paul was not active very long in Antioch before some of the conservative Christians who insisted on fidelity to the Law began to object and raise questions about the legitimacy of his practice. It became such a troublesome issue that Paul went to Jerusalem to meet the apostles to have their judgment about it. The apostles met in what is acknowledged to be the first Council of the Church, *The First Council of Jerusalem*. The history is given in Acts 15.

> Then some men came down from Judea (to Antioch) and taught the brothers: "Unless you have yourselves circumcised in the tradition of Moses you cannot be saved." This led to disagreement, and after Paul and Barnabas had had a long argument with these men it was arranged that Paul and Barnabas and others of the Church should go up to Jerusalem and discuss the problem with the apostles and elders.

> The Apostles and elders met to look into the matter, and after the discussion had gone on a long time, Peter stood up and addressed them. Peter repeated the account of his revelation and the conversion of Cornelius. Following his address, the Apostles reassured Paul and Barnabas that no burdens of the Law would be imposed on the Gentiles.

> The apostles and elders, your brothers, send greetings to the brothers of pagan birth in Antioch, Syria and Cilicia. We hear that some of our members have disturbed you with their demands and have unsettled your minds. They acted without any authority from us, and so we have decided unanimously to elect delegates and to send them to you with Barnabas and Paul, men we highly respect who have dedicated their lives to the name of our Lord Jesus Christ. Accordingly we are sending you Judas and Silas, who will confirm by word of mouth what we have written in this letter. It has been decided by the Holy Spirit

and by ourselves not to saddle you with any burden beyond these essentials: you are to abstain from food sacrificed to idols, from blood, from the meat of strangled animals and from fornication. Avoid these and you will do what is right. Farewell (Acts 15:23-29).

This is a remarkable statement, considering the ambiguity of the Jewish Christians about fidelity to the Mosaic Law. It was an official confirmation of the revelation of God to Peter. "Call nothing profane or unclean which God has cleansed." In view of such a clear and emphatic statement, it is surprising that the issue should continue to be a problem. It reached a point of the sharp confrontation between Paul and Peter at Antioch described in the letter to the Galatians (Chapter 2).

The Confrontation of Paul and Peter

The Church at Antioch continued to flourish, and Galatians 2 describes a visit of Peter to the Church at Antioch.

When Cephas came to Antioch, however, I opposed him to his face, since he was manifestly in the wrong. His custom had been to eat with the pagans, but after the friends of James arrived he stopped doing this and kept away from them altogether for fear of the group that insisted on circumcision. The other Jews joined him in this pretense, and even Barnabas felt obliged to copy their behavior.

When I saw they were not respecting the true meaning of the Good News, I said to Cephas in front of everyone, "In spite of being a Jew, you live like the pagans and not like the Jews, so you have no right to make the pagans copy Jewish ways.

"Though we were born Jews and not pagan sinners, we acknowledge that what makes a man righteous is not obedience to the Law, but faith in Jesus Christ. We had to become believers in Jesus Christ no less

than you had, and now we hold that faith in Christ
rather than fidelity to the Law is what justifies us,
and that *no one can be justified* by keeping the Law."

This was the critical assertion of the "catholicity" of the
Church, the life and way of Jesus Christ as one, but expressing
itself in context of a variety of cultures. Romans who became
Christians were to remain Romans; Greeks were to remain
Greeks; Egyptians were to remain Egyptians. They would live
in conformity to the teachings of Jesus; they would believe in
Him as Lord and Savior; but this belief and this practice were to
express themselves in the way of life of the Romans or Greeks or
Egyptians or others who believe. It was the declaration of religious pluralism in a radical sense. "In my Father's House there
are many mansions." The glory of the Lord's house would be, as
the Psalm said, "surrounded by variety."

Faith in Jesus and Respect for the Law

In view of the clear and emphatic declaration of the apostles
and elders at Jerusalem, it is difficult to understand why the
issue remained a problem in the early Church. But the problem
was to continue during the entire history of the Church. The
confrontation of Paul and Peter took place after the Council in
Jerusalem, a few years after the Ascension of Jesus. It has re-
curred repeatedly in the intervening centuries. It was to be a
major issue at the Second Vatican Council; the remarkable declaration about culture in the Constitution of the Church in the
Modern World is only one of many declarations of the Church
about the issue.

Reasons for the Conflict

Two important factors in human experience were involved
in the origins of the conflict and its continuance. One of them,
profoundly religious, is the experience of religious tradition,
which was particularly important in the life of the Jewish Christians. The second is the basic human experience of resistance to
social change. A common problem in every aspect of human life,
it becomes especially serious when it is related to the continuity

of religious tradition because it then involves the question of the ultimate meanings and values of life.

The Religious Tradition: This aspect of the problem was rooted in the attitude of the Jewish people toward the Law. As indicated above, the only experience the human family ever had with a sacred covenant between God's people and God Himself was the covenant struck by Moses and sealed in the blood sprinkled on the altar and the people, and the Law which was to keep the chosen people faithful to the Covenant and the Promise. This was the basic religious experience and they knew of no other. The sudden replacement of this covenant and the revelation that God's people could be faithful to Him without the Law was a shattering change for the people to understand. It was not that they did not have faith in Jesus. They certainly did; and they knew that belief in Jesus was the way to salvation. But their day-to-day living, the routines of everyday life, the behavior which gave expression to religious truths and values, these were rooted in the provisions of the Law. Briefly, their *culture* was a social expression of the Law. Many of the Jewish Christians knew no practical way of being faithful even to Jesus without respecting and observing the Law. Many of them, perceiving how God was dealing with the Gentiles, acknowledged the freedom of the Gentiles from the Law but continued devoutly to observe the Law in their own lives. For themselves, disregarding the Law would involve a radical cultural change, an experience that is challenging and frequently very painful.

Varying Attitudes Toward the Law

As the Church developed, and especially as increasing numbers of Gentiles became Christians, various attitudes toward the Law developed among the Jewish Christians, and the different attitudes were adopted in one way or another by the Gentiles. The best analysis of these differences is found in the publication of Brown and Meier.[5]

Group One consisted of Jewish and Gentile Christians who were dedicated to the Law and continued to observe it in their Christian life. These were people who saw the tradition as something sacred, the way of life that God had given to their forefathers. It was a tradition that deserved respect. Some of these became over-zealous champions of respect for the Law and were probably the ones who created the problems for the Gentiles in the early Church. Their over-zealous reaction was also provoked by the attitude of some Jewish Christians who rejected the Law.

Group Two were the Jewish Christians and the Gentiles who had a respect for the Law as the great religious tradition of the Jews, but who saw no reason to impose it on the Gentiles. They continued observance of some of the provisions of the Law, particularly the laws regarding food. This is what Brown and Meier call a "mediating position." It was an acceptance of the revelation about the Gentiles, but with a continuing respect for the tradition and those who observed it.

Group Three were the Christians, both Jewish and Gentile, who saw no reason to observe any precepts of the Law. Brown and Meier associate this position with Paul. Paul did not impose on Gentiles the provisions (the dietary laws) that James had asked the Gentiles to observe as a decision of the Council at Jerusalem (I Cor. 10:23-30) although he asserts that he, himself, avoids eating meat (I Cor. 8:13), not because he was a strict observer of the Law but to make sure he never scandalized another by doing so. (Paul's advice to the Gentiles about the problem of eating food that was offered to idols is a model of pastoral counseling.) Differences developed between Paul and Barnabas around the issue of the dietary laws (Gal. 2:13). Brown and Meier (p. 4) state that this may have contributed to the eventual parting of the ways between Paul and Barnabas, although the actual parting took place when Barnabas insisted on keeping John Mark with them on their apostolic journey (Acts 15:36-40).

Group Four were the Jews especially who rejected the Law more openly and spoke critically of its ineffectiveness. Some of the Law-abiding Jews associated Paul with this group, but Paul made it clear that he respected the tradition of the Law and was prepared to observe it (Acts 21:15-26). Group four represented the extreme wing of those who saw no value in the observance of the Law and expressed their opposition to it. Some of the violence that erupted periodically between observing Jews and Jewish Christians was precipitated by the Christians who represented this extreme position.

These varied positions with reference to the Law represented a theological difference, around the significance of the Law as a sacred tradition and a desire to continue it. If the Law were no longer necessary for salvation or fidelity to God, if, as Paul asserted, it was useless for salvation, it was understandable that some Jewish Christians would simply dismiss it and even become critical of those who sought to continue it. A reading of the Gospels and particularly of Paul's epistles indicates how burdensome the Law was. It became doubly burdensome because of the rigid interpretations imposed by the Scribes and Pharisees. A repudiation of the rigidities, severely criticized by Jesus (Mt. 23) could easily become associated with a rejection of the Law itself. It is not surprising that some Jews should have taken this position; what is surprising is that more of them did not do so.

It was the basic reverence for the Tradition that prevailed, not in the extreme sense of an obligation to observe the Law, but a respect for the long religious tradition from which the Jewish Christians had come. It was, after all, their culture. The continuity of the practices, despite the replacement of the Law by the New Covenant, would be expected as a cultural continuity. The great majority of Jewish Christians were impressed by the large number of Gentile converts and their devotion to Jesus; they also were able to accept the assurances of Peter that the Gentiles were to fulfill the obligations of their Faith in Jesus within the context of their own way of life.

The Sociological Problem: The Hebrew tradition of the Law explains to some extent the continuing conflict about the freedom of the Gentiles. There was another factor involved which helps to explain the continuity of the problem throughout the centuries of the Church's life, namely, the consistent resistance to change which is characteristic of all men and women at every stage of history. This is likewise a consequence of culture. The following chapter will provide a detailed analysis of culture, the totality of the ways of thinking, feeling, behaving, and reacting which constitutes the way of life of a people; they are the patterns of behavior which constitute the life of the Japanese as distinct from the way of life of the Italians; the way of life of middle-class Americans in contrast to the way of life of ancient Hebrews or modern Mexicans. Culture is the basic influence in the formation of the personality. In a very real sense, my culture is myself. Therefore, a change in culture involves a profound change of a person's way of life, their personality.

Permeating every culture are the values of a people, and religion is generally the source of the values of a society and culture. Thus the change from the Mosaic Law was not only a religious problem; it was a sociological problem as well. As a sociological problem, it was to reappear in a somewhat different way. It was impressive that God instructed Peter that the Gentiles were not to have Jewish ways imposed on them. History was to reveal, however, that while Christians of each nation (what we would today call each culture) expressed the life and word of Jesus within the context of their own culture, they tended also to identify the faith with their culture. Therefore, when they themselves sought to "preach the Gospel to all nations," while they thought they were bringing the life and word of Jesus, they were actually communicating their own cultural expression of their faith. What they thought was the apostolic sharing of faith in Jesus was in actuality the imposition of their own cultural expression of it on others.

It was a long time before the problem was seen in this perspective. Actually it has been the insights provided by the social sciences into the cultural life of men and women that has enabled the members of the Church, particularly its leaders, to appreciate the basic problem, namely the problem of intercultural understanding and intercultural communication. As Christopher Dawson has expressed it: "Most of the great schisms and heresies in the history of the Christian Church have their roots in social and national antipathies, and if this had been clearly recognized by the thelogians, the history of Christianity would have been a different one."[6] It is the purpose of this book to present some of the sociological insights which may help not only theologians, but all Christians, to understand a bit more clearly the abiding problem of the faith and cultures.

The following chapter provides an elementary presentation of the concept of "culture." It will explain how important an understanding of culture is for anyone who seeks to communicate a religious faith to a person of another culture. It will also help to explain why the revelation to Peter involved such a profound change for the Hebrew people and why the difficulties arose when Jewish Christians realized that the Mosaic Law was no longer the link between God and God's people.

Notes

1. There is a growing literature about the problem of the Church and cultures. Pastoral institutes have developed throughout the world studying local or regional cultures, popular religiosity, and the possible adaptations of Catholic belief and practice to differing cultures. In the United States, one of the best known is the Mexican American Cultural Center (MACC) in San Antonio, Texas, which studies the expression of the faith in Hispanic cultures and the possibilities of cultural pluralism in the Church of the United States. On a more sophisticated and academic level, the Institute for Ecumenical and Cultural Research at Collegeville, Minnesota, is a center for research and publications about the relation of the Church to differing cultures and differing religious beliefs. International conferences occur regularly, such as the conference in the summer of 1985 at Tontur in Israel at which theologians and social scientists discussed the issue of cultural differences and the Church. Where appropriate, reference will be made to relevant publications or conferences. The definitive reference work is *Bibliografia Missionaria*, (Rome: Pontifical Mission Library) yearly. This publishes the titles of all publications about Asia, Africa, Oceania, etc., that appeared in all European languages.

2. National Conference of Catholic Bishops, *The Hispanic Presence: Challenge and Commitment* (Washington, D.C.: U.S. Catholic Conference, 1312 Massachussetts Avenue, N.W., Washington, D.C. 20005, 1984).

3. An excellent presentation of the tension between the Mosaic Law, the Hebrew tradition, and the emerging Gentile Church is found in Raymond E. Brown and John P. Meier, *Antioch and Rome: New Testament Cradles of Catholic Christianity* (New York: Paulist Press, 1983).

4. For a description of Antioch in the time of Saint Paul, see Glanville Downey, *Ancient Antioch* (Princeton, N.J.: Princeton University Press, 1963); or his more popular version, *Antioch in the Age of Theodosius the Great* (Norman, Oklahoma: University of Oklahoma Press, 1962).

5. Brown and Meier, *Antioch and Rome*, "Introduction."

6. Christopher Dawson, "Sociology as a Science," in John J. Mulloy (ed.), *Dynamics of World History* (New York: Sheed and Ward, 1956), p. 31.

2
CULTURE[1]

1. Introduction

The mission that Jesus gave to His apostles was a mission "to the world." "Going, therefore, teach all nations." The world into which He sent them was neither remote nor abstract. It was the busy, active, turbulent, joyful, and sorrowful actuality in which His children were born, grew up, sought to find and fulfill an ultimate meaning in their lives, married, had children, grew old, and died. Within that world, God expected His children to express in themselves the image of Himself created in all of them. It was in their day-to-day activities, their relationships to each other, their effort and achievement, that the spirit of God, living within them, would have to be expressed.

The context of religious belief and practice, therefore, is the total social, economic, political, and cultural reality within which we seek to bear witness to the life and teachings of Jesus. All of these day-to-day activities are touched by the *meaning* people find in their lives. Religious beliefs penetrate this social reality. At the same time, the social reality penetrates the religious beliefs. The beliefs themselves become elements of the total social experience of the people who are members of a particular society.

2. Inculturation of the Faith[2]

This interpenetration of a culture by a religious faith is called in more technical terms: "inculturation." The word of God, the promise of the Messiah, the life of Jesus: these must express themselves in the particular way of life of a people, their social institutions, and their political and economic activities.

27

This interrelationship of all aspects of a society to a set of ultimate meanings and values is called the "culture." Therefore, the study of inculturation is central to a study of the context in which religion is to express itself. A study of inculturation, therefore, must begin with a basic understanding of culture. Culture, very simply, is the way of life of a people. It is the sum total of all those ways of doing things, of thinking about things, of feeling about things, of believing, that make up the life of a group of people. The analysis of a culture will reveal the all-pervading elements which affect religious belief and practice of any society.

Culture is learned in a process of socialization. For example, if a boy were to be born of Irish parents in Dublin and given at the time of his birth to Chinese people in Peking to be brought up, by the time the boy was 21 he would be completely Chinese. He would not be Irish. His features and appearance would be Irish, but everything else — his speech, his way of thinking about things, his way of doing things, his emotional reactions to situations — all of these aspects of his life would be Chinese, not Irish. And he would be as strange and out of place in Dublin as any Chinese child born of Chinese parents and brought up with them. What has happened? In growing up he had assimilated a culture, the culture of Chinese people.

Similarly, a Chinese child, turned over at birth to Irish people to be raised in the Irish countryside, at the age of 21 would be an Irish person. His features and appearance would be Chinese, but in everything he thought and felt and did, he would be Irish. His "Irishness" would influence the way he thinks, the way he deals with people, the way he loves other men and women, the way he relates himself to God.

Therefore, *culture is not race*. Race is biological. Culture is social and psychological. Race is inherited. Culture is learned. The color of a man's skin is a racial characteristic. It is determined by the genes of the organism. But the fact that his color marks him as one of a class of depressed people in a society is not a racial matter at all. It has nothing to do with genes or inheritance. It pertains to the "meaning" that color has in this particular society. This is a matter of culture.

Likewise, *culture is not nature*. Nature is likewise inherited. Culture is learned. There has been a long dispute in many of the social and biological sciences, as scholars attempted to determine what was natural to a person and what was cultural. It is the controversy over heredity versus environment, over nature versus nurture. Few scientists will agree even now on what is inherited as part of a person's nature. All seem to admit that bodily structure, reflexes, certain basic drives to satisfy hunger or thirst are inherited. They admit that some aspects of temperament are inherited, although they are modified noticeably as a child grows up. They admit that some basic capacity to learn is inherited, that by nature some people have a greater capacity to learn than others. But they still are seeking some method that would enable them to determine what this native intelligence is.

Therefore, it is still uncertain just what is natural to a human person. What is not uncertain is the fact that many aspects of the life of a people which are usually considered natural are in fact cultural. People speak commonly of the Irish as being sentimental by nature, of the Germans being practical and efficient, of the Latins being fatalistic, of the Orientals as being unfathomable. The Oriental is not the least bit unfathomable to another Oriental. But the Westerner is as unfathomable to the Oriental as the Oriental is unfathomable to the Westerner. People from the United States often consider Latin Americans devious. But a Latin American is not devious to another Latin American. He is devious only to someone who does not understand his way of life. These are not natural qualities, therefore. They are learned qualities. They have gradually become part of the way of life of a people and they are assimilated by the child who grows up in the presence of that way of life. Bring a Chinese boy up in the culture of Germany and he would learn German efficiency, so that other people would say it was "natural" to him. Bring a German boy up in India and none of the efficiency of the German would be "natural" to him. His characteristics would be those of an Indian. There is a common term which ex-

presses the influence of culture very well. We speak of something as being "second nature," and this is very accurate. For
what a person learned from his culture becomes so deeply in-
grained, so spontaneous, so completely taken for granted that it
appears to be something natural to him.

Culture is like the atmosphere. We live completely immersed in it. We cannot live without it. It influences everything
we think or feel. But we are unaware of it. It is natural for an
ordinary American boy to like sports. He thinks everyone should
feel the same way about them as he does. But he may not have
the same enthusiasm about becoming a ballet dancer. Whereas
Russians have little interest in baseball, but 22 schools select
the best Russian boys and train them for the Bolshoi Ballet.

In discussing culture, there are two aspects of it that one
must learn to distinguish always: the *symbol* and the *meaning*.
The symbol is the thing I see or hear or feel. The more important
thing is what the symbol means. For instance, a man raises his
open hand to his forehead, brings it forward in a sharp and
straight gesture before another man with eagles on his collar,
then brings it down to his side. This is a gesture. What does it
mean? It means respect for one in military authority; it is a symbol of reverence. A second man comes along, raises his open
hand to his nose, places his thumb on his nose and wiggles his
open hand. This is another gesture, very similar to the first.
They are so similar that a foreigner might not be able to tell the
difference. But this second gesture is an insult, a symbol of disrespect and disdain. A person cannot deal with either of these
phenomena, these symbols, unless the person knows what they
mean. And when I know what they mean, I have knowledge of
one aspect of a culture.

It is evident immediately how important in all human in-
teractions is the question: what does it mean? The object or action may be quite indifferent — a movement of the head, a gesture of the hand, a kiss, a tone of voice, a pattern of behavior.
But the action is more than a movement of the head or a gesture
of the hand. It is a movement or a gesture that has a particular

meaning in a particular culture. A man kissing another man on the cheek in France is conveying a friendly greeting. A man kissing another man on the cheek in the United States is inviting ridicule if not suspicion.

Since communication is the conveyance of meaning from one person to another, it is clear how important is an understanding of the culture. For the sum total of "meanings" in the experience of people could be called their culture. If things mean something different to another people than they mean to me, how can I bridge the cultural gap in order to make clear to them what is in my mind? This question becomes critical in the matter of religious communication. "Go teach all nations" involves telling an unbeliever what the life and word of Jesus means. Without an insight into the unbeliever's culture, this becomes difficult, if not impossible.

Meaning and Religious Symbols

Father Andre Dupeyrat, in his little book *Savage Papua*,[3] explains how important the problem of meaning is in the matter of communicating a religious belief or attitude. He explains that among the Papuans, the pig is the sacred animal. So important is the pig, not only as a basic source of food, but as object of reverence, that a woman may nurse a suckling pig at her breast if there is no sow around. In the Hebrew and Christian scriptures, the lamb is the sacred animal. It was the lamb that was sacrificed in the solemn religious rites of the Hebrews. All the religious sentiment associated with the lamb was projected onto Jesus. Jesus is called the "Lamb of God." In order to communicate to Papuans what Christians mean when they refer to Jesus as Lamb of God, Dupeyrat explains that he would have to speak of Jesus as "Pig of God." Therefore to communicate to Papuans the *meaning* things have for people of the West, it is essential to know what things *mean* to the Papuans. This is not easy for persons to do. There is no intrinsic relation between the lamb and the Savior. Jesus was born among people for whom the lamb was a source of food and clothing, the great economic base of their life and their society. And the pig was a scavenger. In the parable of the Prodigal, the son is described as reaching a hopeless state of degradation — he was feeding pigs. The most wonderful thing a Papuan could do is feed pigs. Thus religious meanings become projected in these symbols, economic and otherwise, and they become the context in which our psychological and emotional response to them as religious symbols eventually gets put in place. Take the symbol away and put another in its place and our religious experience can begin to turn upside down. It is the objective of this study to explore the ramifications of this problem of communication across cultures.

Culture could be further analyzed by explaining it in terms of its components: 1) objects or actions which are the visible or sensible symbols; 2) ideas or values which are the meaning of the symbols for me; 3) sentiments which are the emotional reactions associated with the object or action that has a particular meaning for me. It is the interrelationship of all these in the personality that constitutes the effect of the culture on the personality. A few examples may help to explain this more fully.

Eating practices. Americans take it for granted that a knife and fork are the natural utensils for a meal. If you remember the scene from *The King and I* in which Anna tries to teach the King to use a knife and fork, you will recall what silly and inefficient equipment the King thought these utensils to be. In his mind, they could not compare with chopsticks. What sensible person, the King seemed to say, would ever eat with anything but chopsticks? Much more than efficiency are the attitudes and emotions involved. In many Oriental countries, the idea of putting something into the mouth that was already in the mouths of many other people is quite revolting. Chopsticks are better. Persons can reserve their own chopsticks somewhat like Americans and their toothbrushes. One can also break them after eating with them. But Americans, who are probably more sensitive to germs than any people in history, will use in public restaurants forks that have been in the mouths of hundreds of other people. They are making an act of faith all the time that the sterilizing function of the washing machine has been carried out effectively. In all these simple routines of our lives, the objects and actions are intertwined with ideas (of cleanliness and hygiene) and sentiments (emotional reaction of delight or disgust), which reveal that the simple routines are involved in very complicated networks of meaning.

Recently a group of black students from Uganda invited their professors to a dinner in one of the African cultural centers of New York. The guests sat on the floor on cushions and in a small circle. Before the food was served, a bowl of hot water was placed in the middle of a circle. Each of the guests, in the presence of all other guests, washed his hands. The wash bowl was removed; the common dish of food was then placed in the center and each of the guests proceeded to take the food from the bowl with his hands and eat it. The important thing, explained the African students, was the fact that everyone washed his hands in the presence of everyone else. Everyone knew that everyone else's hands were clean. Consequently, there need be no concern about everyone placing his hands in the common food dish. To the African student, this was a much more polite and effective way of assuring cleanliness than our way of assuring the guest that the silverware has been properly washed. These are differences on the most superficial level of culture, but it is clear how important are the meanings that things have and how deeply involved they become with our emotions and sentiments.

Reactions to violence and blood. People of the United States are generally revolted by the sight of blood or violence or death despite the apparent interest in violence and bloodshed on TV and in the films. Ordinarily Americans consider it a barbarous thing to see the body slashed or hacked. It was not so in Elizabethan England. The great event of the week was the public execution. It was not something carefully concealed from the public like our present executions (although the recent presence of TV cameras at executions may suggest a change). Executions in Elizabethan England took place in the public square, in full view. The body was hanged; the genitals were cut off; the intestines were removed; the body was cut into quarters; the head was cut off; and, if the person was important enough, it was set up on London Bridge. The accounts of the death of Saint Edmund Campion (executed 1581) and of Saint Robert Southwell (executed 1595) illustrate this well. These were great public events. And the people cheering the executions on were not barbarians. They were statesmen, lawyers, and divines, graduates from Oxford and Cambridge. They were the people who cheered at the plays of Shakespeare.

This was all a matter of culture, a matter of meaning. Things that would revolt an American audience, that would make people sick, were a grand spectacle then. The same actions had multiple meanings — for the Elizabethan, a public humiliation that a nation's enemy deserved; for the American, a degrading treatment that one would not give to a dog. So, actions interwoven with emotions and sentiments are the different cultures of different people.

Recreation. Another example of cultural definitions could be sought in forms of recreation. Americans in general do not like bullfights. There is blood and gore and the killing of an animal; and, what seems particularly obnoxious to Americans, the bull doesn't have a chance. It is doubtful how many bullfighters would admit that the bull doesn't have a chance. This action or a series of actions certainly has a deep meaning for the Spaniard and excites feelings of admiration, enjoyment, satisfaction. It has a much different meaning for Americans and excites feelings of pity and disgust.

This is not simply a matter of killing a bull. Americans kill bulls much more effectively in a Chicago slaughterhouse. What the Spaniard seems to see in the bullfight is a great human drama, the matching of the rational power of the human against the brute power of a beast. It symbolizes the struggle of the human for mastery over that which is wild. It is this symbolism that stirs the interest of the Spaniard. The preliminaries — the weakening of the bull — are necessary. Otherwise there would be no possibility of a contest. But the first step is the ability of a human to confront that which is wild: not to confront it in any fashion, but with perfect grace, with perfect mastery over self. The willingness to stand within a fraction of an inch of sudden death, and to do this with perfect self-composure, this in itself is a human achievement that stirs the great approval of the

Spaniard. Secondly, the bullfighter subdues that which is wild, brings the bull under his control; gets the bull to stand still, perhaps to drop to his knees. Finally, he imposes a rational pattern of acting upon the beast; leads him one way, then another until the crowning moment when, placing himself in a position of critical danger, he dispatches the bull quickly, gracefully, with perfect finesse. Those who have witnessed what happens to amateurs as they attempt to deal with a bull realize what consummate mastery and skill is involved in this subduing of a wild thing by the reason and skill of a human. In this perspective, the reaction of the Spaniard begins to make sense. His joy at the bullfight is not an indulgence in cruelty or barbarism. It comes from the sensitivity of men and women to the symbolism of human mastery over the brute.

It is important to note here the subtle intermingling of actions, ideas, and sentiments that constitute the human experience of the Spaniard in the presence of a bullfight. This is culture. The bullfight has a meaning for the Spaniard which it does not have for the American. It is only when the American understands what this meaning is that he can begin to communicate effectively with the Spaniard in reference to such a matter. And it is only when the Spaniard understands the meaning a bullfight has for the American that he can begin to communicate effectively with the American.*

Courtship and marriage. A much deeper and more serious level of culture and meaning can be found in courtship practices and marriage. In the United States, for instance, it is a common practice for young boys and girls to mingle socially. They come to like each other, to fall in love, to enjoy a period of youthful romance which usually leads to the moment when they decide to marry each other. The selection of the marriage partner is left to the young man and the young woman involved. Parents or

---

*An interesting conversation of the author with a Spanish friend is pertinent here. The Spaniard was boasting of the superiority of the bullfight over baseball as a human experience. He ended his remarks, "My friend, what real difference does it make who wins a ball game? But what a difference it makes who wins a bullfight!"

advisors may be consulted or may seek to give counsel, but the ultimate choice is left to the couple involved. This seems to American people the most natural and normal thing in the world. They cannot undertand how things could ever be done otherwise. Yet, traditionally in villages in India, for example, the choice of a marriage partner has never been left to the young couple involved. The marriage partner is selected by the parents of the two people involved. It is possible that the girl may never see her husband until the day she marries him. They generally move into the family of the young man if circumstances permit and raise their own family as part of an extended kinship group.

To an American girl, probably nothing is more revolting than the thought of having a husband chosen for her by her parents. She is brought up from the time she is born with the expectation that she will meet young men, that she will fall in love, that she herself will decide whom she will marry. Psychologically, she would probably be incapable of living as a wife with a man whom she had not known. On the other hand, the girl in India would find it terribly distressing if she were told to go out and find a husband for herself. She would not know how to act nor what to do. She has been brought up since birth with the expectation that her parents will choose a husband for her; that older people who are experienced in family life know much better than she who would make a good husband. She is confident that, if things go well, love begins after marriage. She thinks the American girl must suffer terrible anxiety and uncertainty. She accepts her way of life as the best.

Here again is a pattern of behavior, interwoven with ideas, with sentiments and emotions that operate on the deepest level of the human personality. The feelings of the American girl related to her ideas of courtship and marriage are so deep that she could probably never change, and she probably could never bring herself to act against these feelings and ideas. She cannot imagine how a girl in India can possibly live with a husband who was chosen for her. The girl in India probably cannot imagine how a girl can face the problem of seeking a marriage partner for herself. Two cultures are here juxtaposed. Until an American girl understands the meaning that things have for an Indian girl, and until the girl from India understands what things mean to an American girl, there will be no possibility of effective communication between them concerning the matter of courtship and marriage.

These examples have been given in some detail in order to indicate clearly the influence of culture on our behavior; how deeply it affects our personality; how a "way of life" is a subtle intermingling of actions, ideas, and sentiments which reflect the meaning that things have for the people of a particular culture. When persons have been formed by the influence of a way of life, when the meaning of things has become defined for them, they take their way of life for granted. It appears to them to be the natural and normal thing to do. They will be inclined to look upon the way of life of other people as inhuman, abnormal, often impossible. In this state of mind, effective communication with people of another culture is out of the question.

The study of culture, therefore, becomes imperative. In this way men and women can seek to learn, first of all, what people do; they can then try to penetrate to a knowledge of why they do it, to an insight into the ideas, the values or interests that lie behind behavior, the meaning it has for the actors. Finally, they may arrive at some appreciation of the way the others feel when they do act this way. The observers may never reach a point where they will be able to feel the same way a people of another culture feel when they behave as they do. But they will be sensitive to the feelings of the others and they will realize that the others consider their way of life as natural and normal as the observers consider their own. In this way, the framework for communication is created.

This does not imply that as soon as I understand perfectly the way of life of other people, I will approve of it. I may realize that a pattern of behavior in another culture, polygamy, for instance, cannot be reconciled with my own moral principles. The understanding of the culture enables me to appreciate the culture as a human experience of the people who belong to it; it will enable me to judge the behavior of the people who belong to it more soundly within the framework of their total culture. I am then in a position to see clearly its relationship to my own principles, and to appreciate what will be involved if I wish to change the way of life of other people. In other words, I know that which I would like to change before I attempt to change it.

Culture, Morality and Religious Practice[4]

With this background knowledge of the nature of culture, it will be possible to explore in more detail a number of areas in which culture touches directly upon questions of morality and religious practice. Moral judgments are always made within a framework of what something "means to me." And the previous discussion indicates how difficult it is for a person from one culture to appreciate what something means for a person of another culture. Consequently the moral interpretation of another person's conduct becomes extremely difficult. Men and women are always inclined to judge the behavior of other people according to their own way of life. This may lead to unfortunate consequences. For a thing which is morally right in my culture may be morally wrong in another; and what is morally wrong in my culture may be morally right in another. Until I know what an action means to persons in their own culture, I am not capable of passing judgment on the morality of their behavior.

This does not mean that morality is relative in the sense that there are no universal and absolute principles of right and justice. It simply means that all moral principles are relative to the situations in which they are to be applied. A father in the 13th century was certainly not at fault if he did not teach his child to read and write. In those days very few people could read or write and a man could develop himself and participate actively in the social and political affairs even though he was illiterate. A father in the 20th century United States would commit a grave fault if he failed to have his son or daughter learn to read and write, because literacy is essential for a citizen today and illiterate persons will not be able to participate in the social and political life of their society. The example of courtship and marriage in India and the United States illustrates this also. If a father in India fails to provide his daughter with a husband, he would be considered remiss in his duties. In that culture this is defined as one of the serious moral obligations of a parent. If a father in the United States attempted to do likewise and select a husband for his daughter, he would be considered unjust. In the culture of the United States, the girl is considered to have the right to seek and choose her own husband and so any undue interference by parents is considered an invasion of the rights of the child. Consequently, moral judgments must always be made with an understanding of what things mean in different cultures.

One of the most difficult tasks of the scholars in ethics and moral theology is to determine how a general moral principle is related to a particular custom or pattern of behavior in a particular culture. In the following pages, a few examples will be presented of cultural practices to illustrate the importance of relating moral decisions to the meanings that things have in these cultures.

A. *Family Relations*

Chaperonage: Within the framework of moral values, great importance is placed on the chastity of the unmarried girl. Sexual relations before marriage have generally been considered immoral despite the fact that this is being challenged today. This places a responsibility on the parents to provide adequate protection for their daughters. In Latin countries, this responsibility is carried out by some kind of chaperonage. Until the time of marriage, or very close to it, the unmarried girl is never permitted to be alone with a man outside of a protected situation. Either someone else accompanies the couple, or the couple meet in a situation which is defined as safe: in the plaza, at a festival, at the girl's home. People from a culture where chaperonage is common find it impossible to understand the American custom of unchaperoned teenage dating. The idea that an unmarried girl should go, unescorted, to a dance with a young man, should ride alone with him in an automobile, should seek recreation alone with him at the beach or at a ballgame — this is beyond the comprehension of many people in the Latin world. It is defined very decidedly, and by thoughtful and intelligent people, as a lack of moral responsibility.

The person from the United States looks on it in quite a different way. It is expected, in a highly individualistic culture such as ours, that a girl will be taught to take care of herself, that she will be taught self-reliance and responsibility, that she will not need the constant protection of parents or brothers or friends to guard her chastity. Granted the risks involved and the casualties, Americans can cite the experience of large numbers of young men and women for whom the practice of unescorted dating was not an occasion of premarital sexual involvement. Americans in general would consider this a much more responsible practice of morality than the practice elsewhere of never leaving the girl alone.

This illustrates rather clearly the way the same practice can be defined in different ways by two different cultures. And when the definition prevails in a culture, moral judgments must be made within that context. A girl in a conservative Latin American environment, who went off alone with a young man for an afternoon at the beach, would, all things considered, be doing something wrong. Whereas a girl in New York who did the same thing would be doing something quite expected in her way of life. She would be doing something that is morally acceptable.

Husband-wife relations: Relations within the family, relations between husband and wife have been an important concern of moral teachers because the stability of the family depends so much upon this. Yet, there are few areas of moral behavior more directly influenced by cultural differences than relations between husband and wife. In the United States relations between husband and wife are expected to be cooperative, to manifest a spirit and practice of what is coming to be called "togetherness." This is an understandable consequence of a culture in which the individual, whether man or woman, is preeminent; in which selection of the marriage partner is the responsibility of the young man and woman involved; in which man and woman have been given an almost identical education; in which marriage is considered primarily in terms of responsibility to a family. A young woman brought up in the United States is not taught to expect to play a submissive role in her family relationships. She would find it extremely difficult to be left alone with children for a large part of her life, to be told what the family was to do without her having an important say in it, to have decisions made about her life, her children, her home without her being consulted. The morality of a husband's behavior toward his wife in the United States, therefore, is judged with this cultural context in mind. If a husband in the United States compelled his wife to play the submissive role that a woman plays in an Oriental culture, or even in a Latin culture, it is very likely that his action would be called unreasonable beyond limits, and a violation of the rights of his wife.

However, this definition of husband-wife relationships would not apply in most parts of the world. Most families in the world have been patriarchal, in which a wide range of authority was vested in the oldest male member of the family. The same kind of authority was, to a lesser degree, acknowledged in all men who were heads of families. Women have played a submissive role generally. The woman's life was oriented to home and children. She "expected" her husband to be dominant, to tell her what to do, to make important decisions affecting the family, even to discipline her if she did something wrong. Therefore, if the wife is not permitted to walk beside her husband, but must follow him as was the custom in China; if the husband spends a great deal of time outside of the home without explaining to his wife where he is; if he decides that they will move to another area without asking her advice; if he punishes her for not having his meals properly prepared, these forms of behavior may well be defined as moral in the framework of a culture, although they are likely to lead to the break-up of a family in the United States.

Therefore, when a wife is taught to "respect" her husband and the husband taught to "respect" his wife, it is essential to know how respect is defined in a particular culture. The ordinary behavior of a good American wife would strike a Latin woman as a form of great disrespect. Whereas the respect of a Latin woman for her husband would strike a good American woman as a form of servitude. There are certainly universal principles concerning the reverence and respect of husband and wife; but outside of certain basic practices which would be defined as cruel or tyrannical, there are no practices that are universally defined as respectful or disrespectful. One must know the expectations that people learn in a culture before a sound judgment can be made about morality.

The Work of Women: Another illustration of the relationship of culture to moral judgment can be found in the phenomenon of women working, particularly when the woman is a wife and mother. Two conflicting convictions concerning this matter are frequently expressed in the United States: 1) That a woman's place is in the home; that everything should be done to enable the husband to support the family adequately, thereby leaving the wife free to devote herself to the responsibilities of the home. 2) That, in a society like that of the United States, gainful employment outside of the home will be increasingly common for married women. The economic system depends more and more on them; and the small family, the cost of living, and changes in the functions of the family exert a strong influence on the wife and mother to work. Values and ideas should be changed to support the practice of the working wife and mother.

Involved in both these convictions are a great many moral issues, about which moral judgments will be passed. But the moral judgment must always take into account the culture of the people in question.

Women have always worked, and worked hard. It is very possible that women, particularly married women, have consistently worked harder than men. They have tended gardens and tended flocks; they have helped in planting, sowing, harvesting; they have woven cloth and fashioned garments; they have helped slaughter and prepare animals for eating; in India they are hod-carriers and do heavy laboring work; in Africa they handle most of the marketing; in Israel they are soldiers. In one way or other, people in a particular culture determine what is woman's work and what is not. In the United States, the nurse, the typist and stenographer, and the telephone operator are occupations traditionally associated with women. Traditionally in Germany and Ireland, most school teachers were men; in the

United States, on the elementary level, they are predominantly women.

A multitude of factors become involved in the role of women in reference to work. In some of the tribal areas of Africa, it is customary for the wife to keep the garden, to market the crop, and, with her income, to help support her husband. If a man has more than one wife doing this, he may live in grand style. The wife is the one who has the cash, knows how to manage it, how to save, etc., for the welfare of her husband and her home. One of the great problems in Africa arising out of the migration of tribal people to the city is precisely this upsetting of rules. The man gets the wage work in the city; he gets the cash, but he does not know how to manage it for the welfare of the family. The wife, who had been the main contributor of the cash income, now becomes dependent on her husband in a way in which she is not used to. This is having an upsetting effect on family relations somewhat similar to the upsetting of family roles in the United States when a woman becomes the breadwinner.

In the United States, more than 50 percent of all married women with children were gainfully employed according to the 1980 Census. At least 11 million of them were employed full time. This is the adjustment of married women to the rapid changes in their way of life. In the first place, the economic function of the family has changed radically in the past few generations. The home and family were once the center of economic activity, and the wife contributed noticeably to the support and income of the home. She had her own garden, perhaps took care of the small animals, prepared vegetables, and picked fruits and berries and preserved them. In other words, whe was involved continually in economic activity related to the security and prosperity of the family. The important point is the fact that these activities were centered in the home. With the increase in urban living, these economic functions of the woman are transferred to workshop, factory, store, or office. If she is to continue making the same economic contribution, she can do it usually by gainful employment outside the home.

Other economic factors enter the picture also. The increasing demands for education and for better living conditions have placed on the family heavy financial burdens which did not exist before. Economists now indicate that, unless there are two wage earners in the family, it is difficult for the family to meet the economic demands of modern times. Women in the United States are being educated equally with men. Many of them are professionally active before marriage. They seek to maintain that status after marriage, even when they have responsibility for children. Finally, with the trend toward later marriage and smaller families, together with medical care which has lengthened the span of a woman's life, she finds less demand on her time and energy in the home than she once did. All of these factors create the social conditions in which the shift in values has taken place concerning the gainful employment of wives and mothers.

What the married woman in the United States is often trying to do, therefore, when she seeks employment outside the home, is to continue to contribute to the economic strength of the family as she had consistently done in the past. But, in the kind of technological society that exists in the United States, this may be the only way she can do it. Or she may be seeking to contribute to society with the talent she has and the educational training she enjoys.

Therefore, the cultural definition of the work of women and mothers has been shifting rapidly in the United States. This must be kept in mind when one is trying to determine what the gainful employment of a woman means in the United States and, in the context of that meaning, what moral judgment should be passed on it.

Child-parent relationships: Another illustration can be found in relations between children and parents. These likewise become influenced by a culture, and moral judgments must be made with that in mind. The one thing that disturbs Puerto Rican parents when they come to New York is a form of childhood behavior which they define as decidedly disrespectful. In Puerto Rico a child is taught *respeto*, as it is called. This goes much deeper than our American virtue called "respect." It implies an understanding of a child's place in Puerto Rican culture, an understanding of what others expect of the child and what the child may expect of others, and the child's disposition to behave in accordance with this pattern. The child is expected to be docile, submissive, and deferential to those who are older and to everyone in authority. A child's behavior is judged according to these standards. In the United States, however, much greater emphasis is placed on the need to be competitive. Children are expected and are taught to stand on their own two feet, to be self-reliant and independent. The respect of a child for parents is interpreted within this context. But a child behaving in an expected way according to American standards of self-reliance may appear to Puerto Rican parents to be disrespectful. So, they would be inclined to pass an unfavorable moral judgment on this. On the other hand, an American could easily judge a child in Puerto Rico unfavorably because he was not "on his toes," appeared to be too easy-going, or was too pasive about getting things done.

In the traditional cultures of the Orient, for instance, a child, especially a male child, was welcomed as an extension of the family. Great joy attended the birth of the first son because now the perpetuation of the family was assured and the rites of the ancestors could depend on an heir who would continue them. The value of the child is really the child's relationship to the whole family. In the United States, however, children are looked upon in terms of their own development. It is the potentiality of the child himself or herself that is important. Consequently the role of the child will be defined differently.

In an Oriental culture, the child would be schooled into well-defined family roles with emphasis on obligations to the family. In the United States, children are schooled to develop and advance themselves. In the Orient, any advancement of the son that jeopardized his obligations to his parents would be considered immoral; whereas in the United States the personal advancement of the son who leaves his parents alone and "on their own" is likely to be interpreted as part of the American way of doing things. In fact, if parents are too insistent on care and attention from their children and thus interfere with the personal advancement of the children, the parents would probably be criticized for being unreasonable.

It is quite evident, therefore, that the cultural definition of roles will have an important influence on the way people define moral behavior and the way a particular action is considered good, bad, or indifferent.

Modesty: The relationship of moral judgment to culture is probably nowhere more subtle than it is in questions of modesty. Every society makes provision for modesty but they differ considerably. Modesty is a mode of behavior that seeks to avoid sexual stimulation. Immodest behavior or actions or appearances are those things which are designed to stimulate sexual desire in situations in which sexual relations would not be legitimate or moral. Therefore, dress, actions, words, and posture all become subtly defined in different cultures as being modest or immodest. But things that are defined as modest in one culture would be considered terribly immodest in another.

This does not mean that the principle of modesty is relative or indifferent. The principle is perfectly clear: people should not engage in a form of behavior which is sexually stimulating to themselves or others in situations where sexual relations would not be legitimate. What is relative, however, is the definition as to what is sexually stimulating. The dress of American women today in 1980 would have been considered shockingly immodest a century ago. And a very good and modest girl who takes for granted the bathing suit that is quite acceptable at a very respectable beach would have been arrested for indecency if she had appeared in the same kind of bathing suit 50 years ago.

In Japan, for instance, it is quite customary in many of the villages for the entire family to bathe together in the public baths. The situation of parents and children being naked in each other's presence was defined as a perfectly modest situation. Children were brought up to consider it so. And as a result, it was so. An American family would find it impossible to conceive of doing such a thing because, from the time we are babies, we are brought up to define the situation quite differently.

One striking example of definitions of modesty is given by Father Andre Dupeyrat in his book, *Savage Papua*. He describes an incident in which a husband and wife began to argue with each other in the presence of other members of the village. The wife was dressed as all Papuan women dressed at that time, with nothing but a brief loincloth to conceal the genitals. We would have described her as practically naked. In the midst of the argument the husband, wishing to humiliate the wife, seized the loincloth and tore it off her body, leaving her completely naked. This so offended the sense of modesty of the woman, left her so ashamed and embarrassed before her fellow villagers that she could not bear it. She rushed for a nearby tree that hung over a precipice, rushed out on it and threw herself down to her death.

In all these incidents and illustrations, what is involved is not simply a form of overt behavior, but a set of attitudes, feelings, emotions, spontaneous reactions, and associations. When an action or form of behavior becomes generally defined as stimulating feelings of sexual desire, it becomes immodest; when it is associated with spontaneous reactions, emotions, and attitudes that are free of sexual desire, it is modest. It is clear that no two people react the same way to the same things. Therefore, even ordinary forms of behavior in a culture will be more stimulating sexually to one person than they will to another. But beyond that there are certain general tendencies in a culture, common modes of behavior which are considered modest or immodest. Only when observers know these cultural definitions can they pass judgment intelligently about the morality of the actions of people in that culture.

Justice: Finally, a few illustrations can be supplied from the viewpoint of justice. Justice is defined classically as that "virtue by which I am disposed to give every person that which is his due." But what is due to another will be defined differently in different cultures.

In a system of strong family ties and obligations, persons are expected to favor their kinsfolk above those who are strangers. But if a person does this in the United States when dispensing government contracts, administering law, or even dealing in business, the behavior is likely to be definied as improper, as corrupt, and sometimes as immoral. For in the United States, everyone is equal before the law, and each person is to be considered as an individual with certain rights and claims. Therefore, if I have responsibility in a large business for hiring accountants, and I hire my brother who is less competent over a stranger who is extremely competent, in the United States this is judged unfavorably, and perhaps considered immoral. My obligation to my company is to select the best, and not allow family loyalties to interfere with running the business in a most competent fashion. Granted the frequent deviations from this norm, it is still a norm that exerts strong influence in the United States. More importantly, if a person in a public office uses the office to benefit his kinsfolk instead of executing his tasks with expected objectivity, he is definitely considered "corrupt." However, in a culture where family values are supreme and where family loyalties are considered primary, such favoritism to one's kin or family would be much more acceptable. In fact, it could even be defined as obligatory.

These illustrations may give some insight into the deep influence that culture has upon the individual — the way it affects our associations, attitudes, and emotional reactions, and the way it contributes to the formation of patterns of behavior. This is the set of mind, sentiment, and emotion that constitutes the way of a people's life, that makes them satisfied with doing things their way, and that leaves them puzzled and upset when they face the prospect of changing their ways. This understanding of culture should prepare the reader for an appreciation of the difficulties involved in intercultural communication.

The Mosaic Law, Hebrew Culture, and Social Change

The above discussion should throw some light on the problem of the transition from the Mosaic Law to the way Christian life was to express itself in the culture of Romans or Greeks or Egyptians, in contrast to its expression in the context of the Hebrew tradition. Social intermingling with persons of different religious beliefs was not seen by the Romans as a violation of God's law, and the eating of pork or shellfish could be seen as perfectly compatible with a devout religious life. Marriage customs differed among Romans, Greeks, and Syrians; relationships of men to women and of husbands to wives differed considerably. Thus as Christian belief and practice began to express themselves in a Gentile world, they came to be related to differing customs and practices. Symbols that came to convey a sacred meaning emerged from the context of Gentile cultures. A new relationship of the Faith with various cultures began to develop.

This was not without tension and controversy. Many features of life in the Gentile world were judged to be immoral by the apostles and their early followers. Paul's letter to the Romans depicts a society that he defined as very immoral; his letters to the Corinthians likewise portray a society often in conflict with Paul's understanding of Christian virtue. Paul did not hesitate to condemn what he judged to be immoral behavior among the Gentiles while at the same time being firm in his insistence that they not have the Hebrew way of life imposed on them.

As the life and Word of Jesus gradually became "inculturated" into the way of life of the Romans, let us say, Roman life became more Christian as Christianity became more Roman. The interpenetration slowly worked its way out as the influence of Christians increased, but it never reached a point of total integration of religion and culture. Whether in a relatively isolated and marginal situation until the time of Constantine or with the political privileges granted under Constantine, Christian faith and practice found it necessary to relate itself to new political, social, and cultural circumstances. Two very distinct styles emerged, one in the Roman tradition, the other in the Byzantine.

With this new identification of the Faith with distinct cultures, a new set of problems was to face the Church. It was no longer the problem of Jewish Christians having to acknowledge that the life and faith of Jesus could find expression in the Gentile world equally as well as in a Hebrew world. The new problem was the tendency of people of any culture to fall into the common human failing of identifying their way of life with God's law and using their own norms and perspectives to judge the way of life of others. Ethnocentrism, as it is called by sociologists, appeared as a religious problem as well as a social condition.

Communicating the Gospel

In view of this presentation of the concept of culture, the commission of Jesus, "Go, teach all nations," is seen as a more complicated task than first perceived. Communication is a problem of meaning, and meaning is a problem of culture. Commitment to religious beliefs, resistance to social and cultural change, ethnocentrism, and conflicts of interest and struggles for power were all to become involved in the efforts of Christians to communicate to others the teachings of Jesus Christ. Nevertheless, an understanding of culture, cultural differences, and intercultural communication may explain many of the problems which have occurred in history and make it possible to avoid the recurrence of these problems in the present and future. As a background for this, a brief presentation follows of some of the significant moments of the Church's life and an examination of extraordinary efforts to adapt the beliefs and practices of Christianity to the variety of cultures with which it came into contact.

Notes

1. The literature on the concept of culture is abundant. Any good introductory textbook in sociology or anthropology would provide a suitable introduction to the concept and the reality which the concept represents. Clyde Kluckhohn, *Mirror for Man* (New York: McGraw Hill, 1944), and Peter Berger, *Invitation to Sociology* (New York: Anchor Books, 1963), are two of the books widely used to introduce students to the concept of culture. More accessible are the articles on "Culture" in the *New Encyclopedia of the Social Sciences*, as well as in the *New Catholic Encyclopedia*.

2. The term "inculturation" has come to be used in recent years to express the process whereby a religion, for example, Catholicism, is given expression in

a particular culture. The expression of Catholicism within the total culture of India would be an example of "inculturation." It emphasizes the adaptation of the faith to a variety of cultures rather than a process whereby the culture is modified to fit an expression of the faith that is foreign to it. The pluralistic character of the church is emphasized as a consequence of its inculturation in a variety of cultures. See Pedro Arrupe, S.J., "On Inculturation," A letter to the Society of Jesus, *Acta Romana Societatis Jesu* (Rome: Curia of the General of the Society of Jesus, 1979), pp. 256-63.

The journal *Studies in the International Apostolate of Jesuits* published by the board of directors of Jesuit Missions, Suite 300, 1424 16 Street, N.W., Washington, D.C. 20036, frequently publishes articles devoted to the problem of inculturation.

3. Andre Dupeyrat, *Savage Papua, A Missionary Among Cannibals* (New York: E.P. Dutton, 1954). Translated from the French by Erik and Denyse Demauny.

4. One of the best studies of the relationship of culture to moral and ethical judgment is found in J. Langmead Casserly, *Morals and Man in the Social Sciences* (New York: Longmans Green, 1951) Also see Joseph P. Fitzpatrick, S.J., "Justice as a Problem of Culture," *Catholic Mind*, January 1978, pp. 10-26.

3
SOME HISTORIC ADAPTATIONS OF THE FAITH TO CULTURES

A review of some of the most dramatic adaptations of the Faith to foreign cultures will illustrate the problem more clearly and permit a more helpful analysis. The adaptations will be those experiences that have been best known, most dramatic, and most revealing of the problems of relating the Faith to contrasting cultures. The experiences chosen will be 1) the development of the Slavonic Rite by Saints Cyril and Methodius in the ninth century; 2) the remarkable experience of the Chinese Rites, the achievements of the extraordinary Matteo Ricci, and the controversy over the Chinese Rites; 3) the experience of the Spanish missionaries and the religious conquest of the Spanish colonial empire in Central and South America will be discussed in Chapter 5; 4) the problem of adaptation in Africa and Asia, and the increasing interest in "popular religiosity and its importance will be mentioned in Chapter Six.

Each of these experiences requires not one, but many volumes; each has an abundant literature. This chapter is not designed to provide a detailed study of any one of these experiences. They are chosen simply as illustrations, to be presented briefly in order to clarify the problem of relating the Faith to distinct cultures. In each case, the two central issues emerge clearly: "God does not have any favorites," Peter said to Cornelius, "but that anybody of any nationality [culture] who fears God and does what is right is acceptable to Him." Specifically, of what does the fear of God consist and how does one determine

53

what forms of human behavior are "right"? Briefly, what did God tell his followers they were obliged to do? What did it mean "not to call anything profane or unclean which God has cleansed?" At the heart of all these questions is the problem of meaning. What does a particular form of behavior *mean* to the person who is acting? The examples will illustrate the concrete circumstances in which these judgments had to be made, and the problems and controversies which arose as the Church or its missionaries sought to make them.

Furthermore, in no single case is it a religious issue alone. Each case is caught up in a conflict of political or economic or social interests which confuse and complicate the effort to define the religious meaning of the behavior involved. As Christopher Dawson said: "Most of the great schisms and heresies in the history of the Christian Church have their roots in social and national antipathies, and if this had been clearly recognized by the theologians, the history of Christianity would have been a different one."

1. The Slavonic Rite[1]

Constantine (later renamed Cyril) and his brother Methodius were born in about 826 in Thessalonika, a prominent city of Greece. The occupation and activities of their father brought them into contact with the Slavic peoples, and they learned the Slavonic language as children. This proved to be a critical advantage in their later missionary activities. Constantine went to Constantinople, where he proved to be a brilliant student. He was given the nickname "The Philosopher" and later became librarian at Hagia Sophia. Methodius became a monk on Mount Olympus in Bithynia. Cyril followed him into monastic life for a while, later becoming a professor at the Patriarchal Academy of the Holy Apostles in Constantinople. Methodius became the abbot of the monastery of Polychronion in the Hellespont.

In 862, Rastislav, duke of greater Moravia (now part of Czechoslovakia), asked the emperor of Constantinople if he could send some missionaries to the Slavic peoples who would respect their language and culture and understand their desire for political life. The emperor sent Constantine and Methodius. They created a new era for the Slavonic people, inaugurating the Slavonic Rites and beginning a new development in the religious experience of the Slavic people and the Roman Catholic Church. The struggle they faced is a history of religious and political intrigue and conflicts of political, economic, and religious interests, involving suffering, imprisonment, and exile.

The Slavic people had originally been evangelized by missionaries from Ireland and Scotland. More recently they had come under the influence of German missionaries from Bavaria. The interests of the Bavarian missionaries were not only religious. They had political interests as well, hoping through their religious ministry to link the eastern section of Europe to the churches dominated by the German clergy. It appears that there was little interest on the part of the German clergy to adapt their evangelizing efforts to the language and culture of the Slavs. This was evidently the reason why Duke Rastislav sought missionaries who would understand his people and be able to communicate with them in their own language.

Thus the problem of the Church and cultures emerged as a critical issue in the religious life of the Slavs. Constantine was able to take advantage of his early knowledge of the Slavic language; he also created an alphabet so that the language could be written (the alphabet now known as the Glagolithic script). The brothers began to translate the gospels into Slavonic, developed a liturgy in the Slavonic language, and created a form of Catholic practice adapted to the way of life of the Slavic peoples. This program provided the Slavic peoples with a sense of religious identity that supported their struggle for political autonomy.

The experience of Cyril and Methodius raised again the problem of language. Common among the western clergy at that time was a conviction called "Trilingualism" — that only three languages, Latin, Greek, and Hebrew, were legitimate languages for the scriptures and for liturgical rites. The inauguration of the Slavonic Rites created a storm of protest among the German clergy. The legitimacy of language was the symbol be-

neath which a host of political and economic interests were concealed. The western clergy raised a series of vigorous protests to
have the Slavonic Rites condemned and forbidden by the
Church.

It has become clear throughout history that language is not
simply a matter of words. Language becomes associated at the
deepest levels of the personality with attitudes and emotional
responses to social, economic, political, and especially religious
aspects of the life of one or other particular group of people. Thus
the effort of the Slavonic people to retain their rite in their own
language was, as they saw it, a struggle to retain their own iden
tity within the larger body of the Catholic Church. At no time
was there a threat of separation from Rome. One remarkable
thing about the Slavonic Rites is that their participants have always remained in communion with the Pope at Rome.[2] Cyril
and Methodius tried to resolve the issue through dialogues with
the "Trilinguists." But the controversy continued, and the two
brothers responded to an invitation of Pope Nicholas I to go to
Rome to present their case before the Holy See. Pope Nicholas
died in the meantime, but his successor, Pope Adrian II, received the brothers in Rome in 867.

Adrian's response to Cyril and Methodius was very favorable. He solemnly approved the Slavonic Rites and ordained
Methodius a priest. (Up to that time he had been only a monk.)
Adrian ordained three other companions of the two brothers;
and, with high Roman dignitaries present, the newly ordained
priests said their first masses in various churches in Rome, including one at Saint Peter's itself. It was an impressive manifestation of approval and support of the work of Cyril and
Methodius and of their adaptation of the liturgy to the language
and culture of the Slavs in the Slavonic Rites. Shortly after,
Cyril died at Rome on February 14, 869, at the age of 42.

Methodius continued the work alone for the rest of his life.
Pope Adrian II appointed him as papal legate for all Slavonian
people and addressed the bull, *Gloria in Excelsis*,[3] to the Slavic
people, authorizing the Slavonic Rites and placing some conditions on their use and continuance. Methodius was consecrated

a bishop and named to the archepiscopal see of Sirmium in Pannonia. This officially segregated the Slavs from the jurisdiction of the German bishops.

It would appear that this should have settled the matter. It only precipitated a more violent conflict. The German bishops exerted great pressure on the king, Louis the German, to assert himself in the controversy for the defense of the German Church. Methodius was arrested and sent into exile for three years in Swabia, where he was confined to Ellwangen, a former abbey of the German Bishop Ermenrich of Passau. Ermenrich was the leading opponent of Methodius, after the death of Arno of Freising (875) and Adalwin of Salzburg (873). Pope John VIII, through his legate, Paul of Ancona, was able to arrange for the liberation of Methodius in 873. The pope named him a bishop to the see of Greater Moravia.

The progress of the rites continued, but further intrigue began to create more serious problems. Bishop Wiching, the influential leader of the Frankish clergy, became a militant opponent of Methodius. He was supported by the political intervention of Svalapluk, a disreputable successor of Rastislav who showed a preference for the Latin liturgy. This opposition from within his own people and from the successor of the Duke of Greater Moravia who had originally brought him and his brother to the Slavs, was a severe trial for Methodius. Furthermore, as bishop, Methodius found it necessary to rebuke Svalapluk publicly for his disreputable conduct. In 879, Svalapluk was able to exert enough influence to have Methodius called to Rome to respond to two accusations, one a challenge to his orthodoxy (he had omitted "Filioque" from the Creed) and the other for his continued use of the Slavonic Rites. Once again Rome gave complete support to Methodius; and Pope John VIII issued the bull, *Industriae Tuae* (880), unreservedly praising Methodius for his work and confirming the previous determinations of Rome about the independence of the Slavs from the jursidiction of the German clergy. Methodius and the Slavs were to answer directly only to Rome. It is difficult to imagine any more emphatic support for the Slavonic Rites. Again, the bull and the support of Methodius by the Pope only aggravated the conflict further. It flowed over into the political arena and became a crisis of political as well as religious leaders.

The pope, possibly thinking he would resolve the issue, named Wiching, Bishop of Nitra, as a suffragan bishop under the jurisdiction of Methodius. But Wiching kept up his opposition and began to raise questions even in the mind of Methodius about the extent of his jurisdiction. Again the pope settled the issue officially with another bull, *Pastoralis Solicitudinis* (March 23, 881), clarifying the authority of Methodius. The opposition and insubordination of Wiching led Methodius to a point where he threatened to excommunicate him.*

Meantime Methodius was intensely active in his work with the Slavs and the Slavonic Rites. He translated the entire Bible in the short period of eight months. He organized a code of civil law and adapted the Code of Canon Law to the Slavic people. He died in the midst of his labors on April 6, 885. Before his death he had named his own successor, Bishop Gorazd.

The problems of Methodius did not stop with his death. His archenemy Wiching continued his intrigues and used his influence in Rome to have the appointment of Gorazd nullified. In the political order, the hostility of Svatopluk continued. He was determined to undo the work of the two brothers and restore the Latin and the influence of the German clergy. The disciples of Cyril and Methodius were driven out of the country together with Bishop Gorazd and many of the other distinguished bishops associated with the Slavonic Rites.

This appeared to be the end of the great achievement of Cyril

---

*Wiching had a history of deceitfulness in the handling of papal directions. In the case of the pope's firm approval of Methodius, Wiching returned to the court of Svatopluk before the official letters arrived. He distorted the message, giving the impression that the pope had upheld his own (Wiching's) accusations against Methodius, whereas the opposite was true. Again, after the death of Methodius, although the pope evidently intended to appoint Wiching as "acting administrator" of the archdiocese, Wiching informed Svatopluk that he was the permanent and sole successor. (Dvornik, Chapter Six, gives the details of the history.)

and Methodius; actually it proved to be a new beginning. The disciples of the two brothers migrated to the north and spread the influence of Cyril and Methodius and the practice of the Slavonic Rites to the Bulgars, the Bohemians, and the Southern Poles. In 898 the native hierarchy was reinstated in Moravia and the rites were reactivated. It was to be a brief period of relief. Ten years later Moravia was overrun by the Hungarians and a new period of history began.

Analysis

The controversy over the Slavonic Rites is presented here as an example of intercultural difference, intercultural misunderstanding, and a failure to be faithful to the instructions given to Peter: "God accepts any people of any nation (culture) who seek Him and do what piety demands." The discussion of the Slavonic Rites is particularly helpful since it presents the problem in the context of political, social, economic, and religious conflicts of interest, all of which obscure and complicate the fundamental issue that people of a particular culture and language have a right to serve God and to express the word and life of Jesus within the context of their own way of life, providing there is nothing "wrong" about their behavior.

Bitter conflicts were common during the ninth century, not only between the two major segments of the Christian world, Constantinople and Rome, but between emperors, kings, princes, bishops, and many others. Wars were common, and religious conversion was often used to support the autonomy of one political regime against another. In fact, the invitation of Rastislav to Cyril and Methodius to evangelize his people was part of Rastislav's strategy to protect his domain against the German King. The invitation of Boris I of Bulgaria to Photius, Patriarch of Constantinople, to send him priests or monks to evangelize his people, was also related to Boris's desire to be protected against the West. The defense of Cyril and Methodius by Adrian II may have been occasioned by Adrian's fear of the evangelization of the Slavic people by Constantinople. Serious doctrinal issues became involved, such as the use of "Filioque" in the Creed; and deeply rooted ecclesiastical customs got in the way, such as the conviction of the "Trilinguists" that only three languages, Latin, Greek, and Hebrew, enjoyed the privilege as sacred texts; the use of other languages would be a profanation. As a result, the life of the Church moved on, caught in the maelstrom of these conflicting interests, and torn by human jealousy, deceit, and intrigue at all levels, both ecclesiastical and civil.

In the midst of the turmoil of mixed motivations, and the tangle of conflicting interests, there was the effort on the part of Cyril and Methodius to bring the word and life of Jesus to the Slavic peoples in a language and a style that made sense to them, in which they felt at home, in which loyalty to the Church did not mean giving up many of the aspects of their lives which were "natural" to them. The attitude of the German clergy is understandable. They had been brought up in the Latin tradition, in a liturgy that, over the centuries, had become intimately involved in their total way of life. They suffered the common human experience of identifying the Faith, the life and word of Jesus, with their way of life. It requires very careful reflection and a clear perception of language and culture, to be able to recognize the involvement of one's way of life with the practice of the Faith. The Latin liturgy and the western style of religious practice "meant" for the German clergy faithfulness to Jesus and union with Rome. They did not perceive, as Cyril and Methodius perceived, that the Slavonic language and the Slavonic way of life could "mean" for the Slavs what the Latin liturgy meant for the Germans. As indicated above, it is important to note that the Slavs never questioned their union with Rome. It is important also to note the role of the central authority of the Church. It was Rome that saved the Slavonic Rites against all the pressures that were threatening to destroy them.

The Slavic people now face a threat of another kind, the domination of Soviet Russia, a political influence far more powerful than any they have faced before. The issue is no longer that of the validity of the Slavonic Rites as an authentic manifestation of Catholicism. It now becomes a matter of survival in the presence of an atheistic world-view and a political power determined to destroy the Faith in all its forms.

2. The Chinese Rites[4]

Certainly one of the most creative and daring adaptations of Catholic belief and practice to another culture occurred with the development of the Chinese Rites, the adaptations of Catholic belief and practice to the language and culture of the people of China in the 15th and 16th centuries. It was the achievement of a group of Jesuit priests under the leadership of an Italian, Matteo Ricci.

Matteo Ricci arrived in China in 1583, one of the first Catholic priests to penetrate the wall of resistance to foreigners that Chinese maintained at that time. He was never to leave China again. He was to live and work as the most honored Mandarin of this time on a plot of land granted to him especially by the Emperor. He was to be buried with all the ceremonies of Chinese funeral rites, attended by the most eminent scholars of the Court, mourned by thousands of Christians who were the first fruits of his apostolic labors. His biographer described his funeral: "It was less a funeral ceremony than a triumphant celebration, or rather, it was the triumph of Christianity in the Chinese Empire."[5] Another biographer gives a general assessment of Ricci's work:

> In the whole record of cultural contacts it would be difficult to find a period so definitely circumscribed and at the same time so rich in its influence. Jesuit history is not lacking in dramatic chapters . . . but no contribution of the Order is more significant, none has a more important place in the account of human progress than the China mission. Here in a unique and powerful way, the Jesuit was the voice of the East to the West, and also the interpreter of the Occident to the Orient. In this field he stands without a peer, almost without a rival.[6]

In the perspective of this book, Ricci's challenge and achievement represents the most remarkable adaptation of the Church to a new and strange culture. This was a completely different situation from the Slavonic Rites. It was the attempt to bring the life and word of Jesus to a people as strange as any the Church would confront, and with a brilliant history of a civilization rich in the arts, sciences, and social and political organization. It was a civilization as highly developed as any the Church would meet, but a civilization that had closed out foreign influences, that knew little or nothing of the West, and that had never heard of Jesus Christ.

Ricci knew, as he approached China, that two entirely different worlds were going to meet. It was his genius to attempt, in a brilliant but daring way, to make that meeting as beneficial to both worlds as possible. He knew that he was coming to meet a highly developed civilization and a mature and complex culture. He knew he was going to meet a people fully conscious of that highly advanced culture who were firmly convinced that their achievements raised them high above the "barbarous" West from which they sought to protect themselves. He knew that their social system and thier national ideals left them with a proud self-satisfaction and a disdain for anyone from a foreign land.

Ricci also knew something else. He had the sense of a sociologist in realizing that he brought a truth and a knowledge that could challenge the traditional ideals of the Chinese and could shake the social structure of Chinese life. He had the sensitivity to realize the danger of shaking the social institutions of a people before they were ready to shape their lives in a new mold. Ricci was no buccaneer or adventurous merchant intent on selling a product regardless of the effects of novelty on the traditional customs of a strange people. He realized that the powers that drive a society forward lie deep within the human mind and soul and express themselves in social institutions which symbolize for the people the meaning of their existence. It was his genius to attempt to adapt the Catholic faith to the life and culture of the Chinese in such a way that it would not radically disrupt the Chinese way of life, but give it a more creative fulfillment in the context of Christian belief and practice.

Father Orleans in his *Lettres Edificantes* from China describes the situation accurately:

> The zeal of this man, courageous and indefatigable, but wise, patient, circumspect, moving very slowly in order to be more effective, appearing to be timid so that he could take better advantage of opportunities, this must certainly have to be the character of the one God would choose to be the apostle of a Nation so sensitive, suspicious, and naturally hostile to anything that was not born within its borders. . . . But he would have to have a humility and a modesty equal to his scientific knowledge in order to soften the grip of that superiority of spirit of this proud people who would never submit voluntarily, and who would accept something from a stranger only when they were unaware that they were receiving it.[7]

The China of Ricci's Day

China in the 16th century was not only one of the great civilizations of history; its whole life and social behavior were permeated by a set of cultural values called Confucianism. Originally developed by the highly respected sage who lived in the sixth century before Christ, the teaching of Confucius had been elaborated by Chinese scholars, and in the course of history came to be the basic principles of Chinese social life and relationships. Rooted in the virtue of filial piety, the teaching of Confucius emphasized the five central relationships: emperor-minister; father-son; husband-wife; older brother-younger brother; friend-friend. It was the conviction of Confucius that if these relationships were properly honored, social relations would be in perfect order and human life would be fulfilled. The continuing strength and stability of the Chinese family bore this out. The most sacred obligation of every man was reverence for his parents. This became elaborated in extraordinary reverence for the ancestors who had died. The family in its reverence for the dead was seen as the link between the world of the past and the world of the future.

Central to this filial obligation were a set of rituals which had developed around the dead. Burial ceremonies were elaborate. Father Minamiki describes the rites simply and clearly:

Filial piety after death had to be continued in the same spirit as before but in a different form. The personality of the departed was localized in some material substance. A paper object with the name of the deceased written on it was placed before the corpse and accompanied the body to the grave site. After burial the paper object was returned to the home and placed on a small altar where it received the prayers of the mourners. Eventually the paper was replaced by a more permanent form of memorial, the so-called spirit tablet, which was usually made of wood and bore the name of the deceased, the family status, and the person's rank in society. On the back was written the date of birth and death of the deceased. This tablet in some way represented the personality of the departed and carried the inscription *shen wei*, that is, "the seat of the spirit" of the departed. . . .

The unsophisticated people who gathered before the domestic shrine believed that the souls of the deceased were in some way present in the tablets. Under the supervision of the head of the family, the mourners performed various gestures of respect and reverence before the tablets. They knelt and bowed beside the flickering candles, and they burned incense and paper money before the spirit tablets. On certain prescribed occasions such as the anniversary of the death of the deceased or on the first or fifteenth day of the Chinese month, family meetings were held. The family then made offerings of food and drink, placed them in front of the shrine, and later they partook of the offerings in a common banquet. In death, as in life, the family directed acts of obeisance to their relatives.[8]

These rites became much more elaborate among the wealthy

Chinese. Large shrines of the dead would be constructed, and entire clans would gather by the thousands to celebrate the rites to the ancestors on established occasions each year. The *kow tow*, or profound bow, was prescribed. Occasionally animals were slaughtered in the ceremony. Filial piety was directed not only to the dead, but to the living. It governed all social relationships, particularly the reverence shown the emperor.

Together with the Confucian rites, Chinese people had adopted many of the practices of Buddhism and Taoism. These were unofficial and privately practiced in shrines that the followers of these religious practices built and maintained for their practice of Buddhist or Taoist rites. Despite the widespread interest in Buddhism and Taoism, it was actually the teaching of Confucius that ordered and governed Chinese life.

The Approach of the Jesuits

The discoveries of the 15th and 16th centuries opened up a new world to Western Europe: India, Indonesia, the Philippines, Japan, China, Southeast Asia — a bewildering array of people and cultures, highly developed and sophisticated, but with ways of thinking and behaving that were new and strange to Europeans. It was a non-Christian world, and the discoveries set off an extensive missionary effort from Europe to Christianize these pagan peoples.

However, in the intervening centuries, Europe had lost the sense of cultural differences which had guided the Church at the time of Paul and at the time of Cyril and Methodius. Europe had also grown in on itself, and Catholicism had become so inculturated in the society of Western Europe that European missionaries had lost any capacity to distinguish the elements of Catholic belief and practice from the patterns of European culture which they had come to permeate. The early missionaries from Portugal imposed their language on the people of India, had them adopt Portuguese names, and made them follow Latin and a western style in their practice of the faith. Spain imposed its language on the Philippines and likewise transferred to the people of the Islands a western style of religious practice.

The Jesuit founder Ignatius had an entirely different perspective. He was sensitive to differences of language and culture in a way

far beyond that of most of his contemporaries. He insisted that
Jesuits learn the language of the countries where they resided and
follow the manner of living of the priests of those localities. He was
careful to instruct the Jesuits to adapt themselves to the cultures to
which they were sent.[9]

Despite the instructions of Ignatius, the early efforts of Jesuits to
penetrate China were fruitless. In 1565 Father Francisco Peres tried
to obtain authorization to establish a mission in Canton. Chinese officials advised him to go back to Macao and learn Chinese before he
came to China again. A short time later, a Spanish Jesuit, Juan
Bautista Ribiera, set out unaided, unauthorized, and unversed in the
Chinese language or culture to evangelize the Chinese. His experience was such an embarrassment that he was removed from the mission and sent back to Europe. It is no wonder that he failed. He wrote
when he returned:

> During the three years I was at Macao, I did everything
> possible to penetrate the continent, but nothing I could
> think of was of any avail. . . . There is no hope of convert-
> ing the Chinese unless one has recourse to force and un-
> less they give way before the soldiers.[10]

The Jesuit who changed the style and approach of the Jesuits in
Asia was a man of extraordinary insight and intelligence, Alessandro
Valignano. After his initial acquaintance with the Chinese, he referred to them as a "great and worthy people," and he wrote to the Jesuit
General: "The only possible way to penetration will be utterly different from that which has been adopted up 'till now in all these other
missions in these countries."[11]

The first breakthrough came in the person of another extraordinary Italian, Father Michele Ruggieri, who arrived at
the Mission in 1579. He had orders from Valignano to learn how
to read, write, and speak Chinese. He did more than that. He
schooled himself in the manner of life of the Chinese; and, when
he first went to China, he impressed the Chinese so much with
his language and adaptation to Chinese cultural practices that
they insisted on him being present at all public audiences. Ruggieri not only schooled himself. He schooled the Portuguese merchants and government officials to do the same. The Chinese

found him so "at home" among themselves that they offered him unusual favors while he stayed with them. He was proving that China was not impenetrable to one who learned their language and respected their ways. However, he was severely criticized, and not only by members of other religious communities. He was persecuted by his own Jesuit brothers, who accused him of wasting his time. Matteo Ricci described Ruggieri's years at Macao as a kind of martyrdom. The Jesuits there, he said, "although holy men, fail to understand the problem of the Christian mission." Great as was the achievement of Ruggieri, it was to fade in the presence of the much greater achievement of Matteo Ricci.

Matteo Ricci

Matteo Ricci arrived at Chaoching, China, in 1583, in the company of Father Ruggieri. He was 31 years old. He had been born in the town of Macerata, Italy, in 1552, entered the Society of Jesus in 1571, and had the good fortune to study under two intellectual giants of those days: Clavius, an outstanding Jesuit mathematician whose training in science and mathematics was to prove a critical benefit to Ricci in China; and Robert Bellarmine, later a cardinal and canonized saint, whose training in theology and religious controversy contributed much to Ricci's sensitivity to religious differences. In 1578 he was assigned to the Portuguese mission in Goa, India, where he taught for four years. He was ordained to the priesthood in 1580.

At Goa, Ricci came face to face with missionary policies and practices which he considered destructive. Not only were the Europeans imposing western ways on the people of Asia, India, and the Islands. But the Jesuits themselves were advocating a two-class clergy similar to the policy that Spain was following in the Americas. They wanted the native clergy to be given a minimal instruction and assigned as humble, uneducated priests to parishes ministering to uneducated people. Ricci was strongly opposed to this policy and wrote emphatically against it.

Much less should we do so in the circumstances here since, no matter how learned they be, native born Indians rarely receive due credit from whites. . . . Secondly this new policy will encourage ignorance on the part of ministers of the Church in a land where learning is of much importance. . . . Thirdly, and it is this that disturbs me more than anything else, this people have been greatly humiliated in this land. No one has shown them as much understanding as our Fathers. It is for this reason that they have a special love for us. If now they are made to feel that even our Fathers are against them and do not want to enable them to hold their heads high and to make it possible for them to aspire to any offices or benefice on equality with Europeans as education enables them to do, I am very much afraid they will come to hate us. Thus will be thwarted the principal object with which the Society is concerned in India, namely, the conversion of unbelievers and their conservation in our holy faith.[12]

In 1582 Valignano assigned Ricci to the China mission, but commissioned him first to prepare a document describing China for the people of Europe. This was the first reliable report on China to reach Europe. Like the letters of Francis Xavier from Japan, the report of Ricci devoted many pages to the admirable characteristics of the Chinese people, together with a careful assessment of the problems which he was aware of in this unusual culture.

Ricci spent six years preparing himself for his work with the Chinese. He mastered the Chinese language, an almost insurmountable obstacle to Europeans; he became qualified as a Mandarin, passing all the examinations of Chinese scholars; he assembled a large collection of scientific books, instruments, and maps from Europe and set himself up as a scholar, inviting the Chinese scholars to visit with him and learn from him as he continually sought to learn from them. He did not agree with a policy of rapid baptizing of converts. With a sensitivity to Chinese ideals, he recognized that a blending of Chinese and Christian ideals would be necessary, and adaptation of Christianity to Chinese life so that the life and word of Jesus would be given expression within the framework of Chinese culture. He set out to translate the scriptures and Catholic rites into Chinese and looked forward to a clergy that would be authentically Chinese as well as Christian. There would be no imposition of European language and ways on the Chinese Christians.

The Problem of the Chinese Rites

As his mission diveloped, Ricci, as all other Jesuits and Catholic missionaries, had to face the problems that Chinese culture and Confucian ideals posed for Christianity. The most serious was the meaning of the ancestral rites: were these a form of religious worship, or were these to be understood simply as a Chinese manifestation of reverence for the dead similar to the practices in the west of the tombstone, the placing of flowers at the grave, the saying of prayers, the display of pictures, all the ceremonials associated with memorials of the departed soul? Some of the practices in China appeared to a westerner as forms of religious worship. And were the reverences to the emperor an acknowledgement of a divine being or simply a form of reverence to the top ruler of the nation? These were questions that were to be debated intensely for centuries.

Ricci, with his profound knowledge of Chinese life and his insight into the culture, concluded that the rites were not a form of religious worship. Chinese who became Catholic could continue to practice them. Ricci judged that they blended perfectly with the Catholic belief in immortality and the practices in Europe of respect for the dead. He was not to go unchallenged. His decision was to be the center of one of the most prolonged and intense controversies in the history of the Catholic Church.

The ancestral rites were the most pervasive problem. It was the very fabric of Chinese life, touching the life of every Chinese person of whatever age. But there were other problems as well. Ricci had to determine what Chinese term to use in order to convey to Chinese what Europeans meant by the term "God." He wanted to avoid the embarrassment of Francis Xavier in Japan who discovered that he had been misinformed by an interpreter and that the term he was using for "God" was conveying quite a different message to the Japanese.

Ricci approached these problems with an intense searching of the traditional books of the Chinese, and the history of the modifications of the teachings of Confucius by other scholars across the centuries. But he was firmly convinced, by his own studies and his long discussions with Chinese scholars of all types, that the original writings of Confucius did not contain anything that was positively anti-Christian. He was convinced that anything associated with Confucianism in his day that was pantheistic or atheistic was a corruption of the original teaching of Confucius, and that, in attacking the errors of his time, Ricci was simply guiding those scholars back to the purity of their original tradition. Echoing the words of Ricci, Trigault,[13] who translated Ricci's memoirs into Latin, points out:

> Of all the pagan sects known in Europe, I know of no people who fell into fewer errors in the early ages of their antiquity than did the Chinese. From the very beginning of their history it is recorded in their writings that they recognized and worshipped one supreme being whom they call the King of Heaven, or designated by some other names indicating his rule over heaven and earth. . . . They also taught that the light of reason came from heaven and that the dictates of reason should be hearkened to in every action. Nowhere do we read that the Chinese created monsters of vice out of this sureme being . . . such as the Romans, the Greeks, and the Egyptians evolved into gods or patrons of vices.

Ricci believed that many ancient Chinese must have been saved by following the light of their conscience. Trigault continued to question: "This same conclusion might also be drawn from their books of rare wisdom of their ancient philosophers. These books are still extant and are filled with most salutary advice on training men to be virtuous. . . ." However, he points out that the doctrines of these ancient books are no longer held by the scholars of his time.

> The doctrine most commonly held among the literati
> at present seems to me to have been taken from the
> sect of idols, as promulgated about five centuries ago.
> This doctrine asserts that the entire universe is com-
> posed of a common substance etc. . . . This phi-
> losophy we endeavor to refute, not only from reason
> but also from the testimony of their own ancient phi-
> losophers to whom they are indebted for all the
> philosophy they have.

It is clear, therefore, what position Ricci had taken. He was a
master of Chinese language, literature, and antiquities. He may
have known more about ancient Chinese literature than most of
the scholars themselves. And when they protested that his doctrines were opposed to the principles of the Chinese society, he
pointed out to them that Christianity perfected and developed
the truths that formed the original traditions of Chinese life;
that, if any antagonism appeared, it was due to the corruptions
that later interpreters introduced into Confucius; that Catholicism was not out to destroy Chinese ideals, but to restore and
fulfill them and purify them of the corruptions that had crept in.
This approach was not mere opportunism on Ricci's part. He
was passionately convinced that Chinese traditions werre an
admirable preparation for Christianity and that, if they could
be freed from the pantheistic and materialistic interpretations
given them, they would render the Chinese most willing to accept Christianity. The corruptions as he knew them stemmed
back to the writings of Tchou Hi, who attempted to set the teachings of Confucius into a methaphysical framework that was
stifling the real Confucianism from further development.

These statements do not settle the issue of whether Ricci was
or was not correct in his interpretation. The whole terrible controversy of the Chinese Rites was to rage around that very question. But the quotes show clearly the position Ricci had taken in
his effort to prove to the Chinese that Catholicism was perfectly
compatible with the noblest traditions of their nation; that interpretation had left their ideas and ideals in a stagnant
mediocrity; and that, once released from the interpretations,

their ideals would find their noblest expression in Catholic truth.

Intensive studies helped Ricci to resolve the problem of the term he should use for "God." He adopted for Christian use the names *T'ien-tchou*, Lord of Heaven, the *T'ien*, Heaven, and the name *Chang-ti*, Sovereign Lord; he was convinced that the reality represented by these terms among the ancient Chinese writers had many qualities similar to the perfections of the Christian God, and that therefore they could be legitimately used as His name. He could have referred to a long tradition of the Church in doing this, to the difficulties attending the use of *logos* among the Greek peoples and the controversy about the use of the term *persona* in the fourth century. In fact, what could *theos* have meant to the Greeks of the time of St. Paul or Justin Martyr, or the term *deus* to the Romans of the Empire!

It is important to note the influence which the use of these terms had upon the Chinese. J. Brucker, in his admirable article on the Chinese Rites[14] in the *Dictionaire Theologique*, remarks that they had a profound influence not only in drawing the cultured classes to the Faith, but also in combatting the materialism and atheism of the time. He quotes the deputation of the Archbishop of Beryte, whose reports were so important during the controversy that ". . . many of the Chinese were converted when they recognized in their ancient books the fundamental doctrines which the Christians proclaimed."

Ricci's second important conclusion was that the honors paid to Confucius and the great leaders of China were not idolatrous. And that the funeral rites for the dead, either at the time of burial or periodically during the year, purged of the superstitions that Buddhism and Taoism added to them, were not incompatible with the beliefs of the Catholic church. He realized more clearly than many of his successors that the funeral rites were more of a social instrument than a religious rite. As Trigault reports his opinion: "Indeed it is asserted by many that this particular rite was first instituted for the benefit of the living rather than for that of the dead. In this way it was hoped that children, and unlearned adults as well, might learn how to support and respect their parents who were living, when they saw that parents departed were so highly honored by those who were educated and prominent."[15]

It was no secret to Ricci that the Chinese family was the key to the Chinese social system, and he makes it clear that he realized that the funeral rites and ancestral rites constituted the social institution that supported the family system. To cut such a supporting institution from underneath the family system without putting anything in its place would be a serious threat to the stability of Chinese family life. And an outright condemnation of the rites would have done just that. Ricci decided, therefore, that since the rites could be purged of their superstitious elements and could be carried out without any religious content, they should be permitted; otherwise Catholicism would give the impression that it was attacking the traditional structure of Chinese society, a thing which would have been an insult and a sign of unforgivable disrespect for Chinese ideals. Therefore, he permitted the funeral and ancestral rites, leaving it to the Catholic conscience to dictate what should be omitted as a remnant of pagan superstition.

There were other features of Chinese life to which the Jesuits found it necessary to adapt. They had originally worn the garb of Buddhist monks, thinking this identified them as religious men. However, they found that this led to the people confusing them as Buddhists, a thing they wished in every respect to avoid. So they took the advice of their Chinese friends and adopted the dress of the Chinese mandarins. They grew their hair long and shaved their beards; they wore the silk robe of the scholar and wore the scholar's hat at all times, even during the celebration of Mass. The use of dress was the object of lengthy discussions among the Jesuits and only after many consultations did the Jesuit superiors approve of it. It appeared so strange to visitors from Europe that they were accused of disrespect for the Eucharist. Some European visitors brought back rumors that the Jesuits had become effeminate in their style of life.

Ricci encountered a problem in the matter of anointing

people during the administration of the sacraments, since it was forbidden for a man ever to touch a woman. Ricci advised omitting the anointing in Baptism, for this would still leave the sacrament perfectly valid. In Confirmation, however, where anointing is essential, he advised the minister to use cotton held by a tweezer rather than anoint with the thumb as is prescribed by the rubrics. The most serious difficulty came with the sacrament of Extreme Unction, where the anointing of the senses is essential; the priests sometimes omitted the sacrament entirely rather than risk offense, a serious break with Catholic tradition and a violation of the canon law which prescribes the Last Rites whenever they should and can be given. The crucifix was never displayed publicly lest it give the impression of being a superstition. And, finally, instruction about the Incarnation and the Redemption were omitted until the person was about to be baptized. The idea of God becoming man and suffering death for the redemption of rebellious children seems to have been revolting to the Chinese mentality. An effort was made, therefore, to strengthen the converts with the other doctrines of the Catholic faith which would prepare them better to accept the truths which gave them most difficulty. In this matter, Ricci was confident that he was only following the practice of the "Arcana" of the primitive Church, when no reference was made to the Eucharist until the catechumen was ready for baptism.

Ricci set out also to form a native clergy as soon as possible; he translated the Missal, Ritual, and Breviary into Chinese and obtained permission from Rome for the future Chinese priests to use their native language when offering Mass or administering the sacraments. This, however, was a matter of practical expediency rather than an effort to assimilate the Chinese language into Catholic rites. The uncertain position of foreigners in China made the formation of a native clergy imperative. The difficulty of learning Latin was such a barrier to the Chinese students that the use of their native language had to be substituted if a clergy was to be formed in any reasonable time.

This then summarizes the efforts of Father Ricci to bring China to the Catholic faith, but to allow Chinese to remain as completely Chinese as possible when they became Christians. It was the most brilliant and daring attempt at adaptation and assimilation in the history of the Catholic Church. It could be characterized as a clever piece of opportunism, and indeed has been. It could be interpreted as a deceptive attempt to lure the Chinese into the faith. But no interpretation of Ricci's efforts can approach the truth unless it appreciates the motives that guided Ricci's decisions.

He was primarily a saintly and zealous priest who was ready to give his life to assure the salvation of the Chinese people by leading them to Christ. But that was only the beginning of his gifts. His soul stirred with a love of the Chinese themselves. He had been struck with admiration for their achievements in art and culture; he had nothing but eloquent praise for the ideals of their ancient writers. He knew that here, in the soul of China, was no common thing, but a nature endowed by God with extraordinary gifts and bearing within itself the potentiality for achievements of the human spirit surpassing anything that Europe had attained. But he realized also that something was holding that spirit in bondage. The man who had transformed the ethical directions of Confucius into a complete metaphysical explanation of reality had imprisoned in a rigid, inelastic system of ideas the powers of the souls of Chinese that were seeking expression. Now that severe isolation cut off any advance in the sphere of intellect, the Chinese sought a substitute in the emotional satisfaction of the superstitions of Buddhism and Taoism. What Ricci set out to do, therefore, was to save all that he perceived to be great in the souls of the Chinese, to open their eyes to the infinite expanse of revealed truth and, at the same time, to allow them to enrich the Catholic Church with the treasure of their varied gifts, with every usage and custom that could contribute to a better expression of spiritual values. It is beautifully expressed in a passage of his biography:

> From the heart of European civilization, scattered widely in so many manifestations of its activity, from its manufactured products to its intellectual achievements, Ricci wanted to draw everything that ap-

peared to be compatible with the spirit of the
Chinese. His objective was not to impose any unifor-
mity of culture. He remained always respectful of the
distinct features and particular styles of different
peoples, in the hope that all these varied cultures
would find that they could co-exist in the universal
plan of Redemption. In contrast to cultures which are
human creations, limited, incomplete and subject to
error, he saw Christianity transcended by time and
space and, reflecting the light of virtue, presenting itself to all men, accepting them for what they are,
leading them to the mountain that is Christ, but by
different pathways.[16]

Ricci's plans succeeded well during his life. They succeeded for a
long time after his death. But they were destined to be the center
of a long and violent controversy that was to end in tragedy for
the Chinese mission and was to cut off one of the greatest
achievements in mission history.

The Controversy Over the Rites

It would be impossible within the limits of this chapter to go
into any detail about the controversy over the Chinese Rites.
The main lines of the controversy have already been suggested
in the previous pages. The following will merely outline the controversy and then offer a few reflections about the effects of it in
China and the reasons why those effects could not have been
avoided.

About the year 1630, 20 years after Ricci's death, the first
missioners began to reach China from religious orders other
than the Jesuits. When they saw the practices that were tolerated in China, they were deeply disturbed. They sent reports to
their superiors asking for instructions, and a summary of the
difficulties reached Pope Urban VIII in the year 1635. The "die
was cast." It is well to note here that Ricci and his successors
had been in constant contact with Rome. They had submitted
reports on their activities to the Jesuit General in Rome, and
had communicated with the Holy See, receiving officially the
most revolutionary permission for the use of the Chinese lan-

guage in the Mass. The case would probably have been dropped in 1635 because the bishops who had sent the inquiry to the pope admitted shortly after that they had been misinformed.

But, in 1643 a Dominican missioner from China, Father Morales, drew up 10 questions concerning the Chinese Rites and sent them to the Holy See for a reply. The questions were supposed to have outlined the practices in China, and each one ended with the simple query: "Is this permissible?" The pope answered a blunt: "No!" to every one of them, apparently a complete condemnation of the Rites. When the Jesuits in China saw the condemnation, they were appalled. They rushed a priest to Rome immediately to explain that the practices outlined by Morales simply had to be condemned by the pope; he could not have done otherwise. But the practices outlined by Morales did not represent what the Jesuits were practicing and permitting in China. The principles were clear: any permission of pagan superstitions or idolatrous worship, any attribution of pantheistic terms to the name of God, any deliberate concealment of basic Christian dogmas, was wrong and deserved condemnation. The question was one of fact: did this condemnation apply to the Chinese Rites?

If the question could have been considered in its own right, the settlement might have been more rapid and much less disastrous. But once word of the controversy was publicized in Europe, jealousies between the religious orders were injected into it and animosities between the governments of Portugal, Spain, and France became involved, projecting the question into a political background to which it had no reference. The Jansenist movement, with all its bitter hatred of the Jesuits, used the controversy as a tool to turn the sentiments of Catholics against the Jesuits. Everybody seemed ready with an answer; and, as always, the loudest and most intolerant voices were those of men who knew little about China and less about the Chinese Rites. As was the case with the Slavonic Rites, the Holy See responded with great calmness and pursued the question quietly, seeking an objective solution in the face of the violent jealousies and prejudices that were constantly pressing upon it.

Nevertheless, after years of bitter hostility and controversy, in the year 1704 Pope Clement XI issued a final decree condemning the Chinese Rites and demanding an oath from every missioner in China that he would prohibit them among his people. The decree was kept secret for some time, to be promulgated by de Tournon, a special envoy of the pope to China. By 1707, the Chinese emperor learned of the condemnation; it was publicized in China, but with such disastrous results that the missioners decided that the pope could never have meant the condemnation to be applied in such circumstances. Another special envoy was sent to make the proper adjustments to the condemnation. He modified it considerably. But in 1742 Pope Benedict XIV confirmed the complete condemnation of Innocent XI and made provision for its enforcement. The controversy was ended. The consequences were predictable. The Chinese mission was ended also. The result was tragedy.

Anyone with an understanding of Chinese institutions can understand why the tragedy was inevitable. The missioners themselves knew that it was inevitable. It was this conviction that led them to try to evade the decrees when they were first published. In the first place, in the eyes of the emperor and the Chinese scholars, it was a condemnation of the ideals and traditions of Chinese life, a condemnation which a proud and sensitive people could not accept.

> The ancient hatreds of the "pagan foreigners" especially in their writings against Christianity, were not only reawakened; but the great complaint could now more easily be exploited that Christianity preached a disdain for the obligations of Chinese for their parents, their ancestors and the great Teacher of the Nation. Harrassment, as well as persecution, soon broke out on all sides.

The emperor became more incensed at the attitude of the Europeans and was more determined than ever to prohibit the preaching of a religion so openly opposed to the laws and fundamental customs of the Chinese.[17]

Possibly a more serious aspect was that the decision committed the Catholic Church to be, thereafter, a religion of the very
lowest classes if it continued to have any followers at all. It is
true that Christ told his apostles to preach the gospel to the
poor; but if they were the only ones who hear the gospel, especially in a nation like China, the gospel would have very little
influence on the lives of the majority of the people, and its hold
over the lives even of the lower classes would be weak and uncertain. No one could hold a position of influence in China without
pledging his loyalty to the Confucian ideals and paying regular
homage to the master of Chinese society. Once the Rites had
been condemned, the Catholic Church was condemned to a position among the lowest groups. This condition is expressed in
many of the letters similar to that quoted in the *Dictionaire*:

> You ask what impact the new Decree of Pope
> Benedict XIV had on the Chinese Rites? I answer: the
> impact that had to be expected. We have received the
> Decree; we have taken the oath; we will observe it.
> There were not difficulties enough, but now Chris-
> tianity in China has become the religion of a few des-
> titute people who do not have enough to eat or a place
> to live. They are far removed from a status that would
> enable them to make the offerings to ancestors or to
> build a temple. This is the condition of the Chinese
> Christians since the prohibition of the Rites; at least
> for the greatest number. It is absolutely impossible
> for a Chinese Christian, determined to omit the cere-
> monies that have been forbidden by the Decree of the
> Pope, ever to be accepted among the educated people
> without whose influence nothing is given any consid-
> eration, or can prosper or can have any influence in
> China.[18]

This was the end of the story in the 17th century. In the last
analysis, it was the method of the Jesuits that had been condemned. Adaptation and assimilation are remarkable ideals,
but in specific situations, the purity of the doctrine of Christ
must not be risked. The decrees caused a revolution in the

Chinese mission, a revolution that could not have been effected
without disaster. The great majority of 300,000 Christians
would, indeed, have to change a national custom which they had
seen as perfectly legitimate up till then; and in order to change
it, they would have to rout out their most deeply implanted sentiments, break with the most sacred traditions of their country-
men, and as an inevitable consequence, prepare themselves for
the painful persecutions, the loss of their fortunes, and even of
their lives. Faced with the choice, most of the Chinese Christians decided that it could not be done and so the fondest hopes
of Matteo Ricci followed him into the grave.

This presentation tends to create sympathy for the practices
of Ricci and the Jesuits who succeeded him. A word must be said
for the deep sincerity and possibly the deeper wisdom of the men
who opposed the Chinese Rites. Pope Benedict XIV struck the
keynote of their opposition in the conclusion of his bull *Ex Quo
Singulari* when he said: "He hopes that, with the assistance of
God, the missioners would drive from their hearts the vain fear
that by the exact observance of the Apostolic decree the conversion of the infidels would be retarded. For this depends princi-
pally on the grace of God which will not be lacking to their ministry, if they preach fearlessly the truth of the Christian religion
as pure as they received it from the Apostolic See." Even Father
Longobardo, the heroic coworker with Ricci and Ricci's successor as superior of the Mission, disagreed with Ricci's views; but
due to Ricci's influence, Longobardo never interfered with the
practice of the rites. Longobardo

> . . . came to the conclusion that the doctrine of Con-
> fucius and his disciples was tainted with materialism
> and atheism; that the Chinese recognized no divinity
> but Heaven, and the general effect it had upon the be-
> ings of the universe; that the soul, in their opinion,
> was nothing but a subtle, aeroform substance; and, fi-
> nally, that their views as to its immortality closely re-
> sembled a theory of metempsychosis. Regarded from
> this point of view, the customs of China appeared to
> Lombard (Longobardo) . . . as an idolatry utterly in-

compatible with Christianity — criminal acts which must be shown, in their impiety, to the Chinese . . . and which must be absolutely forbidden to all Christians, whatever might be their condition or whatever part of the Empire they inhabit.[19]

But as for the controversy within the Society of Jesus, Pfister adds: "Since everything took place in a spirit of union and charity, and under the direction of obedience, the controversy within the Society never appeared in public and the missionary effort continued as usual.[20]

But as for the controversy within the Society of Jesus, Pfister adds: "Since everything took place in a spirit of union and charity, and under the direction of obedience, the controversy within the Society never appeared in public and the missionary effort continued as usual."[20] Longobardo and the men who agreed with him appreciated very well just what Father Ricci was doing. They saw the possibility of prescinding from religious considerations in the ancestral rites. But their conviction was that, in a nation like China, where the people were so saturated with superstition and pagan practices, you could not permit even the most purified rites without giving the impression that you were permitting superstition. Therefore, the hard and fast line had to be drawn rigorously between everything that suggested paganism and the pure doctrines of Christ.

If this rigid insistence upon pure Catholic doctrine was not enforced, they were convinced, the attempts at adaptation would soon lead to a corruption of Christianity. This was a deep and real fear in the hearts of Ricci's opponents. They could not see the prudence of spending the lives of hundreds of excellent priests on the Chinese missions if their work was to run the risk of preparing a mongrel Christianity that would have suffered the same fate within a few hundred years that Taoism had suffered many centuries before. The danger was too proximate and too critical. They would prefer to stake their lives on a thousand thoroughly Christian souls, rather than expose Christianity to corruption in the souls of a million who could not be trusted. Rowbotham emphasizes this danger very clearly:

The enemies of the order (Jesuit) argued that compromise in such a matter would be deadly to the
Faith. Here, in the light of history, they would appear
to have been on solid ground. It is probable that, had
the Jesuit position been whole-heartedly accepted,
the Catholic Church in China might sooner or later
have lost its identity and become merged in the relatively formless chaos of native philosophical thought.
As has been shown earlier, this was the fate that had
overtaken Nestorianism in China — in which country
the high mysticism of ancient Taoism had also degen-
erated into a system of magic and charlatanry.[21]

And in an admirably balanced judgment of the case, an outstanding Protestant authority on the missions sums up the results of the controversy in much the same way;

... it must be said for the papal decrees that they
helped to keep the Church from losing its distinctive
message and vitality. Had the Church made its peace
with some of the more important existing practices of
China, deterioration would almost certainly have followed. Whatever may be true of the few of the educated, for the great masses the rites had in them
much of animism. It may not be feasible to lead a
people all at once from animism to a pure Christian
faith, but conscious compromise with what is avow-
edly lower and imperfect is dangerous. A Ricci might
safely permit it as long as he was living to guide it,
but under less able and less wise successors it probably would have gotten out of hand. . . . It is conviction
and the sense of values not to be found elsewhere
which in the last analysis must give the Church a permanent place in the community, and if the distinc-
tiveness of its message or its loyalty to truth as it sees
it be compromised, its vitality cannot but suffer. The
papal decisions made the winning of nominal adhe-
rents more difficult, but they tended to keep high the
standards of the Church. Numbers were sacrificed to
vitality.[22]

Later Developments in China

It is not the intention of this book to present an account of later developments in China. The Church continued in China during the 18th century, largely under the care of the Chinese priests who had remained faithful to the Church. As the Jesuits had foreseen, the Church prevailed among the poor peasants in the countryside. Periodically questions would be raised about interpretations of the decrees from Rome. The policies of the bull *Ex Quo Singulari* guided the missionaries in China.

The 19th century brought a change. The Industrial Revolution had taken place in Western Europe; capitalism was developing as an international force; and the period of colonization by the Western powers began to exert itself vigorously in India, Africa, and Asia. China became caught in the process and found itself the victim of repeated aggression by the European nations.

British colonialism in China had actually begun in the late 18th century when the East India Company, looking for new markets, began to push the sale of opium in China. [23] The development of the opium trade began to drain China of its silver resources, and China's resistance to the opium trade provoked a war with England. The Opium War, as it was called, broke out in 1840. Following the defeat of China, England was given trade concessions in China. Other nations, particularly France, followed; and in a short time a number of Western European nations had established stakes in China for the pursuit of trade. The trade was protected by the military presence of the foreign powers, and "compounds" or territories of foreign influence and power became the centers where the presence of the foreign powers were tolerated. Here they conducted their business and lived in a European style under the protection of the armed forces of their native lands.

Regretfully the missionary activities of the Church became associated with the foreign colonial interests. They were granted privileges through the intervention of the colonizing powers and were protected by the colonizing armies. This was hardly the most desirable environment for the reactivation of the presence of the Church in China. Nothing could have been farther from the ideals and achievements of the Jesuits of the 17th century. The "Europeanization" of the Catholic Church characterized the missionary activities of the 19th century.

This period and its consequences are vividly described in the biography of the priest, Father Vince Lebbe,[24] who was one of the great champions in the struggle to de-Europeanize the Catholic Church in China in the early 20th century. There were many devoted missionaries active in China who were not happy about the situation in which they had to work. But since there were some benefits in it for the Church, particularly the freedom to evangelize, they did not take aggressive steps to change the situation. It required the courage and determination of a person like Lebbe to challenge the policies and practices of the Church in China. He was a kind of modern Matteo Ricci. His struggles restored much of the Chinese character to the missions he was involved in. He was largely responsible for the consecration of the first six native Chinese bishops in Rome, on October 28, 1926. He organized the medical services of the Chinese army in its struggle to defend China against the Japanese invaders. He had been dismissed from the Vincentian community of which he was a member and he became a member of the Little Brothers of Jesus. He died in 1940. A national day of mourning was declared in China, and he was given all the honors of a state funeral. He is one of the great missionary heroes of modern times.

The End of the Controversy

Meantime, with the radical changes in Japan, China, and other nations in the Far East, repeated requests were submitted for a re-examination of the decision about the Chinese Rites. On November 19, 1919, Pope Benedict XV published the Encyclical *Maximum Illud*,[25] which called for a new policy for the Christian missions, citing the need for native clergy and native bishops to take full responsibility for the Church in their regions. The letter criticized the "Europeanization" of people to whom the gospel was being preached and appealed for respect for the cultures of these people as they received the teaching of the gospel.

Pope Pius XI moved aggressively to apply the principles of *Maximum Illud* to China. He was the one who consecrated the first native Chinese bishops in 1926. In the same year he also issued an encyclical letter, *Rerum Ecclesiae*,[26] re-asserting the principles of the letter *Maximum Illud*. In 1932 he appointed an apostolic delegate to China with careful instructions that his office was to remain carefully apart from the colonial powers in China. On May 26, 1936 the instruction, *Pluries instanterque*[27] was issued by Cardinal Fumasoni-Biondi, prefect of Propaganda Fidei, making substantial accommodations to the participation of Catholics in the Confucian Rites which were now defined as forms of purely secular reverence for the state or nation.

When Pius XII became pope, he continued the efforts of Pius XI. In his first encyclical, *Summi Pontificatus*,[28] issued on October 20, 1939, he had this to say: "Those who enter the Church, whatever their origin or speech, must know that they have equal rights in the house of the Lord where the law of Christ and the peace of Christ prevail." Finally, on December 8, 1939, an instruction entitled, *Plane Compertum Est*, was issued from Rome terminating the requirement that missionaries to China were to take the oath not to practice the Chinese Rites. The reason for the revocation is clearly stated:

> It is abundantly clear that in the regions of the Orient some ceremonies, although they may have been involved with pagan rites in ancient times, have — with the changes in customs and thinking over the course of the centuries — retained merely the civil significance of piety towards the ancestors or of the love of the fatherland or of courtesy toward's one's neighbor.[29]

The Church forbade any further controversy about the Chinese Rites. Thus, after two troubled centuries, Chinese Catholics could continue to practice the ancestral rites which remain at the heart of the Chinese family life.

But probably the most significant statement from Rome was

issued by Pope John Paul II on the occasion of a conference in
Rome commemorating the 400th anniversery of Matteo Ricci in
China.[30] The Pope expressed his great respect for the genius of
Ricci in adapting himself so completely to the Chinese people
and becoming the instrument whereby European science and
knowledge was communicated to the Chinese and Chinese culture and ideas were communicated to the West. Following are
some of the excerpts from the address of Pope John Paul II.

> Some other Europeans, such as Marco Polo and the
> Franciscans, Giovanni da Montecorvino and Giovan-
> ni di Pian del Carpine, had established contact with
> China in the preceding centuries. However, *Matteo
> Ricci was the first who succeeded in inserting himself
> into the full life of Chinese culture and society*, bring-
> ing to that great People so much of the science and
> technology of Europe, and bringing to the West the
> civilization and the cultural richness of the Chinese
> people. (p. 741, italics mine)

> A contribution of such value could not have been
> made if he had not gone through a long and demand-
> ing period of cultural preparation, and had not ex-
> perienced a profound process of inculturation into the
> reality of Chinese life. Through all of these, Father
> Ricci made a notable sacrifice to learn the language,
> the practices and customs of Cina as if they were nat-
> ural to him. His companion, Father Michele Ruggieri,
> in a letter to a friend, wrote, "We have become
> Chinese in order to gain the Chinese for Christ." (p.
> 741)

> Father Matteo Ricci . . . adopted the style of life of the
> scholars caught up as he was with the social life of
> that community. In this way, he intended to show
> that his religious faith would not lead to any with-
> drawal from that society, but rather to an involve-
> ment in the world in view of the perfection of social
> life up to an opening to redemption in Christ and par-
> ticipation in grace through the Church. (p. 742)

It is surprising that the Holy Father speaks so favorably of the adaptation of Catholic theology to Chinese terminology. As is evident from the preceding pages, this was one of the most controversial issues of the Chinese Rites. John Paul II is emphatic in his praise of the efforts of Matteo Ricci in this regard.

> It was thanks to this kind of an effort of inculturation that Father Matteo Ricci with the assistance of his Chinese collaborators, achieved a task that seemed impossible to work out, that is, a Chinese terminology of Catholic theology and liturgy and, in this way, to create the conditions to make Christ known and to incarnate his evangelical message of the Church within the context of Chinese culture. (p. 743)

> In February of last year, speaking in Manila to representatives of the Chinese communities in Asia, I said: "Right from antiquity the Church has known how to express the truth of Christ, making use of the concepts and adapting itself to the culture of various peoples. The message it proclaims is destined for all peoples and for all nations and is not to be the exclusive possession of one group or one race." (p. 744)

However, toward the end of his address, the Holy Father appears to endorse the missionary methods of Matteo Ricci in a statement that is remarkably clear and emphatic.

> In the light of the spirit of dialogue and of the openness which was characteristic of the Second Vatican Council, the missionary method of Father Ricci appears so much more alive and contemporary. The Decree of the Council, *Ad Gentes (On the Church's Missionary Activity)* seems to be alluding to this when it describes the attitudes which Christians should have: "That they may be able to give this witness to Christ fruitfully, let them be joined to those men by esteem and love, and acknowledge themselves to be members of the group of men among whom they live. Let them share in the cultural and social life by the various exchanges of human

living. Let them be familiar with their national and religious traditions, gladly and reverently laying bare the
seeds of the word which lie hidden in them." (p. 745)

And so he brought to a distant people the faith he had
inherited from his own family and his own people, and
the knowledge which he had gained in the Gregorian
University by making these available to a people enriched by a tradition of deep moral values and a noble
civilization; while at the same time his evangelizing
method contributed to the Church a deep enrichment
of elements of a culture so different, yet in this way re-
fined and perfected.

He succeeded in building between the Church and
Chinese culture a bridge that seems still solidly an-
chored and secure, despite the misunderstanding and
the difficulties of the past which keep coming back to
us. I am convinced that the Church can guide itself
without fear along this path, with its eyes pointed toward the future. (p. 745).

The Chinese Catholic Church

This was the end of one kind of trouble. Another was to break
upon the Church within very few years. After the Communist
domination of China in 1948, many of the bishops in China, yielding to the pressure of the Communist leaders, broke with Rome
and established the Independent Chinese Catholic Church. The
bishops and priests who remained faithful to Rome have been sub-
jected to harrassment, persecution, and imprisonment. Some have
died as a result of their suffering. Thus the problem of adapting
the Church to the culture of China takes a new and possibly more
difficult turn. The future still remains a mystery while Pope John
Paul II seeks to establish friendly relations with the people of
China and their government in the hope of one day finding a re-
medy for the sad division of the Church which now exists.

Analysis

The contact of the Church with the culture of China in the

17th century will probably remain the most serious challenge the Church has ever had in the matter of intercultural understanding and intercultural communication. From a sociological point of view, the culture of China was so deeply rooted in the society, had such profound meaning for the people of China, and so thoroughly penetrated the whole fabric of Chinese life politically and economically that resistance to change would have been almost unshakeable. The missionaries who understood China realized this. The ancestral rites were so much a part of every aspect of Chinese life, representing that which was holy and sacred. They were also the basis of the fundamental value of family loyalty. They gave life its meaning. The removal of the rites would have meant the complete dismembering of Chinese society.

If there was little likelihood of any change in the matter of the ancestral rites, the question remained for the missionaries: to what extent can Catholic life and teachings be accommodated to the practice of these rites? "God has no favorites; he accepts anyone of any nation (culture) who seeks Him and does what piety demands." What did piety demand in the case of the Chinese Rites? Ricci, with his remarkable mastery of the Chinese language and his equally remarkable knowledge of the Confucian classics, together with his long association with the intellectual and political leaders of the Chinese people, made the judgment that the rites were social and cultural and were not a form of religious worship. Others, many of whom unfortunately knew little about China or the rites, did not agree. But, as is evident from the passages above, some very knowledgeable people had serious doubts about Ricci's judgment.

The change in the official position of the Church took place only after the governments of Japan and Manchukuo* provided statements that the rites were a purely secular gesture, honor-

---

*Manchukua was a section of China, overrun during the 1930s by the Japanese, and later established as an independent nation. The first government statement about the character of the rites came from the government of Manchukuo, and the first response of the Church modifying its position about the rites (1938) was issued on this occasion.

ing the family and the nation. They had no religious significance. It is interesting to note that the Church was willing to accept the official assurance of the governments; to what extent is
this a more accurate definition of the situation than the assessment of a profoundly learned scholar such as Ricci? Furthermore, Ricci had the advantage of being thoroughly familiar with
Catholicism, whereas the Japanese and Manchukuan governments were not. Was not Ricci a more reliable witness than the
governments?

The difficulty of judging the religious issue was complicated
both for the Chinese and the Church by the political and commercial interests which were entangled in the process. The aggressive attacks of the European powers in the 19th century indicate why China was concerned about the threat of Portuguese
merchants, backed up by military power and seeking to legitimate their activities by pretending to be a Christianizing force.
Had the situation permitted the religious problem to be
examined carefully in its own right, the ultimate tragedy might
have been avoided. As in the case of the Slavonic Rites, the conflicts over political and economic power confused and clouded
the issue. Misjudgment was inevitable.

Finally, there was the conflict among the missionaries themselves about styles of evangelization. This appeared not only between Jesuits and Franciscans; it appeared among the Jesuits
themselves. Ricci found it necessary to defend himself against
those who considered his type of apostolate useless. They were
committed to a direct preaching of the gospel to the people, proclaiming the life, death, and resurrection of Jesus. The idea of
spending years in a scientific salon in conversations with intellectual leaders and serving as consultants to the Chinese Emperors on matters such as the calendar struck them as a waste
of time. However, the fruits of Ricci's ministry were proof of the
validity of his methods. The thousands of Christians, many of
them the most influential people of their cities and regions, were
ample proof that the gospel could be brought to a people like the
Chinese through the secular interests in which they were involved.

It is not likely that a situation such as that of China will confront the Church again. Persons inside and outside the Church in this generation are much more sophisticated than the people of Ricci's time about the involvement of culture in religious and social life. The problem, however, emerges on other levels, on the level of parish or neighborhood, where persons of different cultural backgrounds meet. An understanding of the Chinese Rites and the problems created for the Church by this controversy can alert both the faithful and the officials of the Church to the need for intercultural understanding and the basic skills of intercultural communication. This will not automatically settle the issue, but it will create a situation in which an approach to a settlement may move with less hostility and better understanding.

Notes

1. The best available history in English of the development of the Slavonic Rites is found in Francis Dvornik, *Byzantine Missions Among the Slavs*, (New Brunswick, N.J.: Rutgers University Press, 1970). Much of the present brief review is based on this book. A more accessible source but nowhere near as complete, is the article, "Cyril and Methodius" in the *New Catholic Encyclopedia*. The recent encyclical of Pope John Paul II, *Slavorum Apostoli* (Apostles of the Slavs) *Origins*, Vol. 15, n. 8 (July 18, 1985), also has a brief history of the brothers and a reflection on the nature of their work. It also has a selected bibliography. In a previous encyclical, *Egregiae Virtutis* (Dec. 31, 1980) *AAS* 73 (1981) pp. 258-262, Pope John Paul II had proclaimed Saints Cyril and Methodius co-patrons of Europe.

2. This is the experience singled out for great praise by Pope John II. It is an example of a church which kept its own identity and autonomy while remaining faithful to the Roman church and the church of the West.

3. See Dvornik, p. 147 for a discussion about the authenticity of this bull.

4. One of the best books in English about the Chinese Rites is the remarkable history of the China mission in the 17th century by George Dunne, S.J., *Generation of Giants*, (South Bend, Indiana: University of Notre Dame Press, 1962). This is an eminently readable book as well as a work of careful scholarship. Two recent publications have added to the available literature in English. One by George Minamiki, S.J., *The Chinese Rites Controversy* (Chicago, Illinois: Loyola University Press, 1985) is the best complete review of the controversy from beginning to end. The publication of Jonathan Spence, *The Memory Palace of Matteo Ricci* (New York: Viking, 1984) is focused on the techniques of memory of Ricci, which enabled him to astonish the Chinese by his extraordinary feats of

memory. But in the process, Spence gives a wonderful presentation of the life and work of Ricci as a missioner.

5. N. Trigault, *De Christiana Expeditione Apud Sinas*, quoted in L. Pfister, *Notices Bibliographiques* (Changhai, 1932), p. 32.

6. A.H. Rowbotham, *Missionary and Mandarin: The Jesuits at the Court of China* (Berkeley: University of California Press, 1942), p. vii.

7. Pierre Joseph d'Orleans, S.J., *Lettres Edificantes de Chine*, quoted in Pfister, *Notices*, p. 33.

8. George Minamiki, *The Chinese Rites Controversy From Its Beginning to Modern Times* (Chicago: Loyala University Press, 1985), pp. 5 and 6.

9. See Pedro Arrupe, "Inculturation: A Letter to the Whole Society of Jesus," in *Acta Romana Societatis Jesu* (Rome: Curia of the General, 1979), p. 261. Arrupe gives the references to the Constitution and letters of Ignatius.

10. Dunne, *Generation*, p. 16

11. Dunne, *Generation*, p. 17

12. *Ibid*, p. 25

13. L. Gallagher, *The China That Was*. An English translation of the Introduction of Nicholas Trigault's Latin Translation of Ricci's memoirs, pp. 154 ff.

14. J. Brucker, "Chinois (Rites)", *Dictionnaire de Theologie Catholique* (Paris, 1932), Vol. II, Part 2, Column 2389, probably the best treatment of the Rites from a theological point of view.

15. Nicholas Trigault, *The China that Was*, translated by Louis J. Gallagher, S.J. (Milwaukee: Bruce, 1942), p. 159.

16. Henri Bernard, S.J., *Le Pere Mathiew Ricci et la Societe Chinoise de San Temps* (1552-1610, Tientsin, 1937), Vol. I, p. 366.

17. *Dictionaire de Theologie Catholique*, Ibid.

18. *Ibid*., Col. 2389.

19. L'Abbe Huc, *Christianity in China, Tartary and Thibet* (New York, 1857), p. 199.

20. Pfister, *Notices*, p. 61.

21. Rowbotham, *Missionary*, p. 296.

22. K.S. Latourette, *Christian Missions in China*, (New York, 1929), p.154.

23. See "China: The Opium War" in the *New Encyclopedia Britannica*.

24. See the remarkable biography of Pere Vincent Lebbe, *Thunder in the Distance*, by Jacques Le Clercq (New York: Sheed and Ward, 1958).

25. Benedict XV, *Maximum Illud*, November 20, 1919, *Acta Apostolici Sedis* (1919), pp. 440-455.

26. Pius XI, *Rerum Ecclesiae*, June 15, 1926, *Acta Apostolici Sedis* (1926), pp. 65-83.

27. Propaganda Fidei, *Instructio: Pluries instanterque*, May 26, 1936. *Acta Apostolica Sedis*, 28 (1936), pp. 406-9.

28. Pius XII, *Summa Pontificatus*.

29. Propaganda Fidei, *Plane Compertum Est*, December 8, 1939. *Acta Apostolici Sedis*, 32 (1940), p. 32.

30. Pope John Paul II: "Address to the Participants at the Gregorian University on the Occasion of the 400th Anniversary of the arrival of Fr. Matthew Ricci in China" October 25, 1982, in *Acta Romana: Societatis Iesu* (Rome: Curia of the General of the Society of Jesus, 1983), Volume 18, #3, pp. 740-747.

4
THE AMERICAN EXPERIENCE

The history of the United States offers one of the most impressive examples of the intermingling of people from many different cultures into one politically unified society.[1] The motto of the United States, *"E Pluribus Unum,"* seeks to express this. On the religious level it brought together people from many different religious backgrounds, most of them Christian. On the level of the Catholic Church, it brought millions from different cultural backgrounds of Catholic life and experience. Thrown into contact with each other, facing the task of understanding each other, they have molded a common nation and a common society out of an extraordinary array of differences.

At the center of this experience was the Catholic Church. Catholics had been a samll, rather elite group of colonists in the days before the American Revolution (1775-81). Some of them played a prominent part in the founding of the new nation. Charles Carrol of Carrolton, a distinguished Catholic, signed the Declaration of Independence. His relative, John Carrol, became the first bishop of the new nation. But the experience of the Church in America emerged with the coming of millions of Catholic immigrants from Europe, mostly poor and uneducated people. They came from different cultural and language backgrounds: Ireland, England, France, and Germany, and later from Italy, Poland, and the nations of Central and Southern Europe. It was the adjustment of these immigrants to the United States and to each other that was to constitute the unique experience that developed in the Catholic Church in the United States.

The adaptation of the Church to culture was to face a new challenge. It was to find itself in a new world unlike any it had lived in

95

before. It was an expanding world in which modern technology, industry, and commerce were to emerge with extraordinary suddenness. It was a world in which political institutions of freedom and opportunity were vital realities for the first time in history. Into this world the Church arrived in the form of the millions of immigrants from Europe. In the midst of these new and challenging circumstances, it faced the task of giving a new and creative expression of the life and word of Jesus.

The history of that experience has been written by numerous excellent historians[2] and has been analyzed by theologians. The task of this chapter is not to review or summarize or evaluate the excellent accounts and studies of the period. Rather it is to examine the process of what is called cultural assimilation and the way the Church influenced the process and was influenced by it, in other words, the response of the Church to its contact with the culture of the United States. Thus it will be rather narrowly sociological, but with a practical focus; to provide a perspective on the present and future challenges to the Church that remain in its contact with the United States. This may provide some helpful guidelines for persons who must guide the life of the Church. One thing is clear in the accounts of the previous century: the Church made some regrettable mistakes which could have been avoided. A clearer perspective on that past may help the present members of the Church to avoid similar mistakes in the future.

The Coming of the Immigrants

The 19th century and the first 20 years in the 20th century were the period of massive immigration from Europe. Between 1820-1920, at least 40 million immigrants came to the United States from Europe. Taking only the largest groups gives some idea of the size and diversity of the movement:

Country	Year	Total Immigration	Peak Years
*Germany	1820-1975	6,917,090	1881-90
Italy	1820-1975	5,269,637	1901-10
Ireland	1820-1975	4,720,427	1850-60
Great Britain	1820-1950	4,386,692	1881-90

**Austria-Hungary	1820-1950	4,172,104	1900-10
***Russia	1820-1950	3,343,895	1910-20
France	1820-1975	740,000	1850-60
****Greece	1871-1975	629,278	1911-20
****Turkey	1971-1975	282,023	1901-10
Poland	1820-1950	422,326	1910-20

*Includes Jews born in Germany.
**Changes in political boundaries make accurate counts impossible.
***Includes Jews born in Russia.
****Most immigrants from Turkey were actually Greeks.

Source: Reports of the United States Immigration and Naturalization Service.

The migrations came in three major periods. The early migration (1780-1860) came mainly from northern and western Europe — from Great Britain, Ireland, Germany, and France. Since Quebec, Canada, was still French territory, most French immigrants settled there; since Canada apart from Quebec was still part of the British Empire, many immigrants from Great Britain also settled there. But the great numbers came to the United States. Large numbers of French and Germans were Catholics, but the great number of Catholics came from Ireland.

The immigrants from Ireland were poor peasants. They had lived for two centuries under oppression by England. Catholics could not own land; if they attended school, they were instructed in the Anglican faith. The price of fidelity to their faith was life in poverty and oppression. They began to leave Ireland in large numbers in the late 18th century; the migration continued in the 19th century and became a rout when the potato famine (1846) left millions dead and dying. Uneducated, unskilled in husbandry, poor, and in weak health, they endured the inhuman conditions of travel to the United States on converted lumber and fish boats. British physicians who accompanied some of the ships wondered how any of them survived. As one doctor remarked: "If you placed a wooden cross on the Atlantic Ocean for every Irish person who died in passage, you could pave the Atlantic with a wooden highway from Cobh to Boston and New York."

The Irish were deeply devoted to their faith. They also brought with them extraordinary skills in political organization which enabled them, despite persecution and discrimination, to rise to political power in the cities where they settled.

The Germans were much better off. Many of them were craftsmen. They were also in better health and strength. Together with the Irish, they were to constitute the rapidly growing ranks of Catholics in the United States.

The so-called new immigration (1860-1920) brought people from eastern and southern Europe: Italians, Jews, Poles, and natives of Austria-Hungary, Russia, and Greece. These arrived in the United States about the time the earlier immigrants had become settled and established. The new immigrants, therefore, faced a United States whose life and culture had already been affected by the experience of millions of earlier immigrants.

In 1924, fearful that the immigrants would become a corrupting influence in the United States, the predominantly Anglo-Saxon citizens passed a very restrictive immigration law which limited the number of immigrants entering the country.[3] All Asians were excluded; the act provided for 165,000 visas per year, assigned on the basis of nation origin — two percent of a nationality's number in the country in 1920. The act was designed to favor immigrants from Great Britain, Ireland, and Germany, and to restrict immigration from central and southern Europe. This quota system was discontinued in 1965.

The third wave of immigrants came after the second World War. Between 1945-55, half a million refugees and displaced persons came from Europe to the United States. Between 1959-61, 600,000 refugees from Cuba came to the United States; these were followed in 1980 by 130,000 Cuban "boat people" — a panic exodus of poor Cubans together with occupants of prisons and mental institutions that Castro dumped onto the United

States. Between 1975-80, close to 600,000 Vietnamese refugees were settled in the United States. Refugees together with legal immigrants have constituted an average of 600,000 newcomers per year in recent years.

Many of the newcomers are legal immigrants who are admitted under the immigration legislation of 1965. This legislation eliminated all quotas, did away with all exclusion based on nationality, and provided 290,000 visas, available to anyone anywhere in the world who meets the conditions established for legal entrance to the United States. Each nation is limited to 20,000 visas on a first-come, first-served basis.

Together with the immigrants, a large number of Puerto Ricans have come to the mainland United States.[4] They are American citizens by birth and face no restrictions on travel to the mainland. However, they come from a different language and cultural background from most mainland Americans and they face many of the same problems of adjustment as immigrants from foreign lands.

Together with all these legal newcomers are large numbers of so-called illegal immigrants, persons from foreign countries who are present in the United States without any documents providing for legal residence. They come largely from Mexico, Central and South America, and from the Caribbean. Many are Spanish speaking, part of the new population which will be discussed in Chapter 5. Many are refugees from Central America, particularly El Salvador, Guatemala, and Nicaragua, where hostilities have driven millions from their homes.

The Challenge to the Church

The Church faced two major challenges in the presence of this experience: 1) how to relate to the dominant society and culture of the new nations, namely the predominantly Anglo-Saxon, Protestant culture which had formed the nation before and after the Revolutionary War;[5] and 2) how to deal with the variety of Catholic groups which were coming in large numbers to the nation — Irish, French, German, English, Italian, Polish, Slovak, Lithuanian, Hungarian, and many other smaller nationality groups. There were also large numbers of Catholics of Eastern Rite churches who had come to the United States.

Reaction to the American Political and Social Environment

For the first time in its existence, the Church found itself in a nation dedicated to religious freedom, but guaranteeing that freedom to all religious groups. It was a religiously pluralistic society. This created problems on the theological level and on the level of practical political and social policy.

There was no theological tradition in the Catholic Church that was capable of responding to the situation of the United States. In the European theological tradition, the concept prevailed that only the true religion had the right to a protected position in the political order. The argument unfolded very simply: Jesus Christ had revealed the true faith to the world, and this was to be brought to the whole world through the Catholic Church under the successor of Saint Peter, the pope at Rome. No government had the right to provide protection or freedom to a religion which, by definition, was false or untrue. A theological position firmly related to the American experience was not to be officially accepted by the Church until the Second Vatican Council when the Decree on Religious Liberty was officially proclaimed.[6]

Despite the problems of the theological tradition, the experience of the Church was leading to new perspectives on the nature of the Church and its relation to a democratic society such as the United States. Dolan described it as follows:

> Thus, by 1790, a unique vision of the church was beginning to surface in the United States. The republican blueprint envisioned a national, American church which would be independent of all foreign jurisdiction, and would endorse pluralism and toleration in religion, a church in which religion was grounded in intelligibility and where a vernacular liturgy was normative, and, finally, a church in which the spirit of democracy permeated the government of local communites.[7]

Once the Church became organized in the United States, the emerging concept of an "American" Church came under attack. It was not long before the concept of the Church on the European model became dominant. In other words, bishops were to be appointed by Rome; the liturgy would be in Latin; the hierarchy would exercise religious authority; the European tradition would continue in the United States. When the large numbers of Catholic immigrants began to arrive, this tradition became even more secure. It presented the Church as the immigrants, and particularly the immigrant clergy, knew the Church in Europe.

The experience of the Roman Catholic Church in the 19th century was anything but ecumenical. It met with severe hostility. It was seen as a foreign religious influence in a democratic society; Catholics were accused of having a loyalty to the pope, a foreign potentate. There was a widespread conviction that they could not accommodate themselves to a democratic society with religious freedom such as prevailed in the United States. During the entire 19th century Catholics suffered persecution, discrimination, and public vilification, particularly because of their religious beliefs and practices. The response of Catholics to this hostility was a vigorous assertion of their loyalty to the United States and to the principles of religious freedom. They simply asked that the religious toleration so loudly proclaimed be extended to them as citizens of the nation. This turbulent and hostile situation resulted in a muting of the theological issue because of the more immediate demand by Catholics for recognition as loyal citizens.

Despite the hostility, the Catholic immigrants found a nation of religious freedom and social and economic oppportunity. They were among the very poor. But the Irish, for example, had religious and political freedom that they had not enjoyed for two centuries under English rule. They took advantage of their political freedom. Moving quickly into political life, they displayed a remarkable skill at political organization. They gained political control over Boston and New York by 1870. They used their political skills to secure their religious rights. Together with the developing nation, they also achieved remarkable improvement in their social and economic position.[8]

Thus the first objective of the Church in the United States was to claim for itself the religious freedoms guaranteed by the Constitution. This required political organization and political action of a determined kind. It was largely the Irish political leadership which proved significant in this struggle. The experience of Archbishop John Hughes of New York is a striking example of the political struggle which eventually secured the rights of Catholics as free citizens of a free land.[9]

It was this historical experience of Catholics in a religiously pluralistic nation, rather than any theological debate, which resulted in an adaptation of the Church to a religiously pluralistic society. Catholicism flourished in this new environment, despite the hostility; and it was clear that a doctrine of "separation of Church and State," with a guarantee of freedom for all religions, was a political and religious environment perfectly adaptable to Catholic life and practice. Eventually, in the Second Vatican Council, it was the pragmatic experience of the Church in the United States that proved to be a decisive argument for the legitimacy of religious pluralism as an acceptable Catholic position.[10]

However, a third aspect of American democracy was rejected, namely the democratic election of pastors by lay trustees and the election of bishops by the local clergy. Both of these ecclesiastical adaptations to American democracy were strongly encouraged by clergy and laity and a few bishops. But the conservative tide in the Church in the early 1800s prevailed, and the authority of the bishops was asserted: pastors would be assigned by bishops and bishops would be appointed by Rome. Thus what developed was a strange blend of ecclesiastical authoritarianism and American democracy, the exercise of religious authority in a Church that enjoyed religious freedom in a religiously pluralistic society in which a separation of Church and State was officially proclaimed and enforced. What was developing was a new Catholic culture, the adaptation of the Church to a new political and social reality. It was to prove a healthy environment in which the Church would grow. The Church took maximum advantage of its new found freedom.

The National Parish

While it was achieving this new creative adjustment to life in the United States, the internal problem of the Church remained to be faced, namely, the diversity of Catholics from different language and cultural backgrounds in Europe. Irish Catholicism differed from German Catholicism not only in language but in a variety of customs and practices which had developed in the cultural environment of Ireland rather than Germany. The response to this by the Church in the United States was the national or language parish.[11] In other words, apart from the conventional territorial parish, a parish defined by geographical boundaries (everyone within certain boundaries belonged to Saint Mary's parish, for example), special parishes were created for members of a particular language and cultural background, German or French (and, later on, Polish, Italian, Hungarian, Slovak, Ukrainian, etc.). This was possible mainly because large numbers of clergy and religious came with their own people in the migrations. As a matter of course, the German priests established German parishes for the Germans; the French did likewise. Later on the Italians, Poles, and others would follow this example. Thus a large diocese of the United States would consist of a mosaic of territorial and national parishes under the jurisdiction of the bishop. Consequently the organizational structure of the Church reflected the "*e pluribus unum*" (unity in the midst of diversity) ideal of the nation at large. The national parish was to play a central role in 1) the process of assimilation of immigrants to American life; 2) the unity of the Church; and 3) problems of political control within the Church.

The National Parish and Cultural Assimilation

The problem of cultural adjustment, as we have seen, has been a longstanding problem in the history of the Church. But it was generally a problem that developed in the evangelization of new populations — the mission to the Gentiles in the time of

Paul, the mission to the Slavs in the time of Cyril and
Methodius, the adaptation of Catholicism to Chinese culture in
the Chinese Rites, etc. But, now, for the first time, the problem
was to occur in a different context, in the convergence of Catholics of many cultural backgrounds in a newly developing world
which guaranteed religious freedom. The problem emerged
around the continuity of the cultural differences in the national
parishes in relation to the dominant culture of American society.[12] Briefly, were the Germans to remain Germans or were
they to become Americans, whatever that might mean; were the
Poles to remain Poles or the Italians, Italian? This was the problem of cultural assimilation and the role of the national parish
in the process.

Cultural Assimilation[13]

The American experience precipitated a problem which was
to trouble the United States for many years, namely, the
"Americanization" of immigrants. To what extent were the
newly arriving immigrants to change their culture and accept
the dominant culture of the United States and to what extent
were they to seek to continue to live according to the culture
from which they had come? Recall the problems of cultural differences discussed in Chapter 2. Once a person has been
socialized in a particular culture, it is a profound change for the
person to seek to accommodate to another different culture.

The influence of the Anglo-Saxons had created a nation with
a decidedly clear culture, an open-class society which provided
the opportunity for upward social mobility and guaranteed all
citizens the right of access to these opportunities.[14] It emphasized the independence of each individual and the right of
the individual to compete for advancement. It provided educational benefits to prepare citizens for participation in political
life and for their own social advancement, not to be held back by
ties of family, ethnic origin, race, or religion (an ideal that faced
serious resistance and that was realized only after constant
struggle). The nation guaranteed due process of law and jury
trial. It was proud of these achievements of a democratic society
and was determined to perpetuate them.

When newcomers from areas that were not Anglo-Saxon arrived, the reaction of the Americans was to demand that the newcomers adopt the values and culture and style of life of American people. This was particularly troublesome to Catholic immigrants since the Americans tended to identify American values with the Protestant tradition from which their people came. But the problem went beyond the religious issue; it touched the issue of language, social custom and tradition, and values and interests which were part of the way of life of Germans or French or Italians and others.

The immediate reaction of newcomers to this pressure was resistance. They had come to America not to surrender their values and way of life, but to enjoy the freedom to be themselves in a new and free world. They tended to cling to their values in groups that became the familiar immigrant communities of American cities — the little Irelands, or Germanies, or Italies, where people of the same language and culture clustered together in ethnic neighborhoods where life continued in a familiar way and where the newcomers felt at home. For Catholics, the heart of these immigrant communities was the Catholic parish. Thus the parish and the immigrant community became a transfer of part of the old world to the new. It provided a continuity that cushioned the shock of transfer to a new and strange world and became the basis for a sense of social solidarity which preserved a sense of identity among the newcomers. In the course of American history, it became clear that the immigrant community, far from hindering assimilation to American life and culture, was the social institution that made it possible by making the transition more gradual and more peaceful.

Actually what happened was a three-generational process: by the third generation the grandchildren of the immigrants had largely lost their language, had assimilated American ways, and despite remnants of the old culture, were actually indistinguishable from Americans of other cultural backgrounds. Americanization had occurred not the way the early Anglo-Saxons had expected, quickly and abruptly; but rather more effectively, as a gradual and peaceful process.

Assimilation and Catholics

The process of assimilation took place among Catholics as well as others. The parish served as the heart and center of the immigrant Catholic community. But by the third generation the grandchildren had lost the language and, to a large extent, had moved elsewhere, largely to suburban areas where middle-class Americans clustered. An interesting phenomenon had occurred. The Church of the immigrants had become Americanized with them, taking on the characteristics of middle-class America. It was by the mid-1900s a decidedly American institution. The election of John F. Kennedy to the presidency in 1960 is seen as the turning point of the American Catholic experience, the moment when it appeared that Catholic immigrants had come of age and were accepted as true Americans by the American people. A new Catholic Church emerged from the process; a new manifestation of the faith within a new and distinct American culture, with characteristics quite different from the cultures of the nations from which the immigrants had come.

Seeking a New Cultural Expression of Catholicism

The Americanization of the Catholic Church (the three-generation process into middle-class America) has not solved the problem of the relationship of Catholicism to American culture. It has left the Church with a new set of problems to face. In the assimilation of Catholic immigrants into the mainstream of American life, the Old-World cultural supports of the faith have largely been lost. For more than a century the strength and stability of the Church rested on the cultural supports which the immigrants brought with them. Now, as these supports weaken and disappear, there is nothing in American culture which provides a similar support for Catholic belief and practice. Furthermore, the culture of the United States is itself in a period of convulsive change. For example, traditional family values experience severe strain:[15] the formation of small children suffers from the gainful employment of mothers outside the home; the high rate of divorce and remarriage among Catholics is a serious challenge to the Church; traditional values of chastity are battered by the sexual revolution and the impact of new permissiveness; there is widespread resistance of Catholics to the official teaching of the Church on birth control; public policy protects abortion on demand. All these create a climate of uncertainty and ambiguity in the effort of the Church to identify the behavior which reflects the fulfillment of Catholic values and ideals. This experience of Catholics simply reflects the profound social and cultural changes which affect most societies in the world. But with the loss of the Old-World cultural supports and the uncertainties of the emerging culture of the United States, the Church faces a challenge as severe as any it has faced in history.

All this has occurred, of course, at the very time when the consequences of Vatican II have affected the traditional practices of the Church. The loss of conventional practices which were once the identifying symbols of the Catholic has left the faithful confused. The lack of vocations and the loss of clergy and religious; the shift in emphasis from a triumphant Church to a pilgrim people; the appearance of disagreement among theologians about the basic teachings of the Church; the new ecumenism — these have all contributed to an uncertainty within the Church itself which handicaps the Church in her attempt to respond positively to the contemporary world. The visible signs of the Church as a presence that permeates people's lives has weakened. The main indicator of fidelity, namely attendance at Sunday Mass, had dropped from 66 percent of all Catholics in 1966 to 40 percent of all Catholics in 1976. Whereas noticeably more Catholics than Protestants were at Church every Sunday in the mid-60s, 10 years later, they were much closer to the same level.[16] Greeley notes that the percentage has remained at that level for the past 10 years.

The struggle of the Church to find a suitable cultural manifestation of Catholic life became more and more important, yet difficulties were to hamper the Church along the way. It would seem that the changes in U.S. culture would leave openings that Catholicism could fill. But this would require creative ability and courage, qualities which were to fail at a critical moment.

The National Parishes
and the Unity of the Church

The national parishes played another important role: they maintained a strong link between the diverse Catholic cultures of the immigrants and the centralized church. They served not only as the basis for the stable immigrant communities, giving the immigrants the strength and sense of identity which enabled them to move with a sense of security into the mainstream of American life. They also retained the diversity of the Church in such a way that the unity of the Church on the diocesan level was never threatened. The national parish had its own cultural style of Catholicism, but it was under the jurisdiction of the bishop; the unity of the diocese was a unity in diversity, a mosaic of Catholic differences constituting a unified whole.

The importance of this became clear when the one great threat to this unity arose in the form of a demand by German immigrants for separate national dioceses as well as parishes. If this had occurred within the same city, for example, Boston, there would have been eight or 10 dioceses, each nationality group with its own bishop. The Church saw in this the possibility of harmful fragmentation. The leader of this movement was a German layman named Peter Paul Cahensly.[17] Cahensly had been very active with German Catholic immigrants, providing orientation to them before they left Germany, assistance for their journey, and a helpful reception when they arrived in the United States. This assistance to Germans was remarkably well organized and served to reinforce the sense of identity and stability of the German Catholic immigrants. The German parish was the center of much of this activity. It was understandable that Cahensly and the other leaders should think of German dioceses as well.[18]

The American bishops, including conservatives such as Archbishop Michael A. Corrigan of New York, stood firmly against this plan. Despite the strong clamor of the advocates of national dioceses and their influence at Rome, Rome supported the American bishops in their opposition. The national parish was seen as an important response of the Church to the diversity of immigrants; the national diocese was seen as a threat to the unity of the Church.

The problem of cultural assimilation was very much involved in the plea for national dioceses. The nationality groups demanding it were convinced that the loss of the Old-World language and the Old-World culture would result in the loss of faith of millions. There was some basis to their argument. The strength of the Church actually rested in the national cultures which the immigrants brought with them. It was understandable that their participants should think that when the whole cultural context of the faith was lost, the faith would be lost with it. This was indeed the issue involved in the problem of cultural continuity vs. assimilation to the culture of the United States. Would the faith survive if the Church became American?

The bishops who advocated Americanization saw the situation differently. Their primary concern was political: the importance for the Church that Catholics should be seen as true and loyal Americans. They were convinced that the Catholic faith and American democracy were compatible and that the Church should rejoice in the religious freedoms of the United States and take advantage of them for its own welfare. But there was much more to it than citizenship and national loyalty. The United States was rooted in a framework of values that were very different from those of the Old World: a focus on the importance of the individual; an open class society in which the individual could compete for higher socio-economic status; a society dedicated to universal education; a democratic society providing for free election of representatives, where freedom of speech was guaranteed and due process was a constitutional right. Persons formed in this cultural environment would not have the same attitude toward the Church and its institutions that European immigrants had. If Catholics became assimilated into the American culture described above, would the faith survive with them? Many of the bishops were convinced not only that the Church would survive, but that it would prosper in the American environment.

Actually a process ensued which neither group clearly

foresaw. The national parish provided the cultural continuity and the sense of identity and solidarity that the first-generation immigrants needed. Without it, they would have faced the dangers of a life troubled by social disorganization and insecurity. The national parish gave the immigrants the strength from which they moved with confidence into the mainstream of American society. In the presence of an English-speaking world, the second generation immigrants began to lose the language; by the third generation, the grandchildren had intermarried extensively with persons of other nationality backgrounds, had adopted middle-class American ways, and, to a large extent, had moved to the middle-class suburbs of the large cities. In the process they had not lost the faith; rather they brought the Church into the American middle class with them. The old cultural Catholicism had been lost, but a new style of Catholic life had emerged which reflected the values and practices of the middle class. But as they sought to give expression to the Faith in this new cultural environment, the problems of middle-class American life began to create difficulties of its own.

A study of the development of Italian parishes provides another example of the role of the national parish in the assimilation of immigrants; it also clarifies the relationship of the national parish to the over-arching diocese. The author, Father Silvano Tomasi,[19] sees the Italian parish almost as a sect, a relatively isolated group with their own customs, practices, and fiestas, a neighborhood that was really an Italian village. The role of the parish in providing a sense of identity and cultural continuity has been described in detail.[20] Yet, through the priests and their relationship to the bishop, the parish linked the Italian community to the larger world of the American Catholic Church. This prevented the parish from becoming an isolated segment, and so the diocese served as a mediating institution through which the parish remained in a vital relationship with the unified Church. The unity never became threatened. The assimilation of Italians was even more pronounced than that of the Germans. As a Mediterranean people, they were far more distant from the Anglo-Saxon character of American society.

Nevertheless, by the third generation the same process of cultural transition had taken place. Italians had become middle-class Americans. In the process, far from losing the faith, their practice took on the characteristics of middle-class American Catholicism.

The Problem of Power

There was another agenda involved in the controversy about national parishes. It was not a matter of culture but a problem of power in the Church. The dimensions of this were much clearer and more realistic. By the close of the 19th century, the Irish dominated the dioceses of the United States.

> In 1900 bishops of Irish birth or descent were presiding over such key dioceses as New York, Boston, Baltimore, Philadelphia, Saint Paul, and San Francisco. In fact, two-thirds of all the bishops of the United States were of Irish descent; even in the diocese of Saint Louis, where the clergy of German descent outnumbered the Irish, all but one of the twelve St. Louis priests promoted to the episcopacy between 1854 and 1922 were Irish. Other immigrant groups resented such domination, and before long the Irish became the common enemy of non-Irish immigrant Catholics.[21]

Dolan also indicates that, by 1900, 15 percent of the bishops were of German background. But the Poles "who mounted the strongest campaign for bishops, ultimately failed. . . . The immigrants wanted power and control but were unable to gain it." In the New York Archdiocese, where Italians outnumbered the Irish by 1920, the first Italian to become a bishop was Bishop Joseph Pernicone, in 1953. And he was only an auxiliary bishop in the archdiocese.

In brief, the same political skill that brought the Irish politicians to power in the major cities of the nation also brought the Irish clergy to power within the Church. In a sense it was the working out of the immigrant experience within the Church. The Irish were on the scene first, and with large numbers of clergy. As the Church grew, they grew with it, and they used their sense of power to control it.

Thus power became another dimension of the adjustment of the Church to a new cultural situation. What the Church would do and how it would do it would depend to a large extent on those who controlled it. For better or worse, this was the Irish clergy. As it turned out, there was little unanimity among them about the response the Church should make to the American experience. The early emphasis on an "authentically American" Catholic Church reasserted itself during the 19th century. Bishops like John Ireland of Minneapolis-Saint Paul and John Lancaster Spalding of Peoria, Illinois, were strong voices appealing for an extensive accommodation of the Church to American values and culture; conservatives like Archbishop Corrigan of New York and Bernard McQuade of Rochester were wedded to a European concept of the Church.

The conflicting opinions were strongly expressed around the controversy about "Americanism." Briefly, this was an accusation by European and especially Roman clerics that the Church in the United States was characterized by a spirit of individualism, of personal freedom, of a sense of continuing progress, of an adjustment to the emerging world of industrial progress and democratic political institutions. These values, so deeply rooted in the American style of life, were seen by Europeans as incompatible with the true values of Catholicism. American Catholic life was condemned as a new "Pelagianism" — a spirit that placed control over human destiny in the hands of the men and women of the world and saw little need for reliance on God's providence.

Central to the controversy was Father Isaac Hecker, a distinguished convert and founder of the Paulist Fathers. Hecker died in 1888. A biography of Hecker by Father Walter Elliot, C.S.P., published in 1891[22] and presenting an organized account of Hecker's beliefs, precipitated the problem. Hecker represented in his personal life and his published opinions the main features of "Americanism." He saw the Holy Spirit actively involved in historical events and insisted on the importance of in-

dividuals listening to the promptings of the Spirit. He encouraged more active involvement of the laity in the life of the
Church. He saw the qualities of American life as the unfolding
of human life under the impulse of the Spirit. In his eyes, if the
Church would learn to respond positively to American values, it
would gain the world of the future. To those concerned with the
interests of the institutional Church, the words of Hecker left
them "trembling," as one writer put it.

The debate about national dioceses and national bishops became entangled in this problem. The advocates of the German,
Polish, and Italian Catholics, the critics of the domination by
Irish bishops, tended to phrase the controversy as an effort on
their part to preserve a true European style of Catholicism (that
is: without the German language and German culture, the faith
of the people would die); whereas they claimed the Irish bishops
were allowing the Church to be dominated by American values
and an accommodation to American interests.

Indeed, some of the Irish clergy were promoting the values
of American society. Bishop John Keane, rector of the Catholic
University of America, Archbishop John Ireland, Bishop John
Lancaster Spalding, and James Cardinal Gibbons in Rome,
were bringing the message to Europe where, among liberal cler-
gymen and scholars, they were heard with great attention.
Archbishops Corrigan and McQuade were among the conservatives, including Jesuits in Europe and the United States. It was
still a problem of the assertion of the centralized authority of the
pope in Rome or the accommodation of Church authority to democratic institutions of the United States. The arrival in 1892 of a
Roman visitor from the Vatican, Archbishop Francesco Satolli,
gave the appearance of Roman support for the Americanist position. Conservatives were dismayed when Satolli remained in
the United States as the first apostolic delegate. The conservatives were relieved, however, when Satolli changed his position
and took a firm stand against the main ideals of the
Americanists. The controversy in Europe became intense with
the publication of the French translation of the biography of
Father Hecker. Hecker was presented as the ideal example of

American spirituality. Followers of democracy in France saw
the account of Hecker's ideas as a model for the French Church.
Royalists "maintained that it contained the seeds of heresy."
Hennesey believes that when the Royalists and conservatives
were really opposing was Hecker's support of the "active individualism, self-confident mystique, and optimistic idealism of
American civilization."[23]

In any event, the American values were officially condemned
in an encyclical letter of Pope Leo XIII, *Testem Benevolentiae.*[24]
It effectively put an end to the effort of forward-looking clerics to
bring the Church into the modern world. Both Hennesey and
Dolan see it as the sad mistake that stopped the development of
the Church in midstream. "American Catholics had known an
inchoate moment of native constructive theological thought,"
writes Hennesey, "they now slipped more or less peaceably into
a half-century's theological hibernation.[25] As Dolan summarizes it,

> The spirit of independence articulated by Carrol, En-
> gland, Hecker, Ireland, and others disappeared.
> Novelty and pluralism were cast aside in favor of
> order and discipline, Rome had become not just the
> spiritual center of American Catholicism, but the in-
> tellectual center as well. This put Catholics in a
> strange stance, they were both 100 percent American
> and 100 percent loyal Roman Catholics to the core. It
> was a unique blend of religion and nationalism which
> most other Americans failed to understand.[26]

Continuing Assimilation

Whatever the condemnation of Americanism did, it failed on
two accounts: the Irish bishops remained in control of the
Church and the process of assimilation of Catholics continued
in full flood. The Church became middle class American. It was
not the dynamic, forward-looking Church that Ireland, Keane,
Spalding, and Gibbons had hoped for. But it was not the Church
envisioned by the Europeans. Instead of giving direction to the
changes in American society, the Church simply adapted itself

to the ongoing process of the development of American society. As Will Herberg[27] puts it, it accommodated itself itself to the dom-
inant values of the United States. Instead of calling God to witness to the activities of American life, it lost its prophetic thrust and conformed to the "world" as it was unfolding in the American experience. It now faces the range of problems which the American experience presents to it. The cultural innovation which Ireland, Hecker, and others hoped for may not now be possible. But the Church still faces the challenge of finding a new cultural expression of Catholic life, a pattern of ideas and behavior that reflect in the contemporary world the vital presence of the Church, the spirit of Jesus in our midst.[28]

Religion and Culture:
The American Experience — An Assessment

With reference to the problem of religion and cultural differences, what does the American experience have to teach us?

1) *The continuity of religious faith is not necessarily affected by profound cultural change.* The Catholic Church in the United States, even in the presence of the difficulties it is facing, is still a strong Church, the expression of a strong faith within the context of American society. The change in the cultural context of Catholic life and practice in the American experience has been deep and extensive. The fears that the faith of the immigrants would be lost if the language and cultural background of the immigrants was lost proved to be unfounded. Furthermore, and American Church on the model of John Carrol or Archbishop Ireland or Father Hecker was never actually developed. As Dolan describes it, a strange amalgam developed of a Church with decidedly American middle-class characteristics, but completely loyal to Rome and responding generously to the leadership of the Roman pontiff, a blend of nationalism and Catholicism which most non-Catholic Americans do not understand.

2) *The religious pluralism of the host society was a critical factor in the process.* Despite the hostility, prejudice, and discrimination from which the Catholic immigrants suffered, the

basic institutions of the new society held firm. Religious freedom and religious pluralism were the rule of the land. The hostility was not capable of weakening the faith of the immigrants in the presence of the institutions which guaranteed its freedom. Thus the immigrants were able to move into the mainstream of the new world and bring their faith with them. Becoming American did not imply the surrender of one's faith. In other words, the religious pluralism and separation of Church and State constituted a political climate favorable to religious change.

3) *A gradual transition was possible.* The host society permitted the continuity of the variety of language and cultural backgrounds of the immigrants. had they been uprooted abruptly from their culture, the shock would have affected not only the faith of the newcomers, it would have created problems for the host society. What acctually occurred was that the religious continuity provided a basis for social solidarity and security. The clusters of Irish or Germans or Italians or Jews in the immigrant communities provided the "position of strength" from which the immigrants moved with confidence into the mainstream of American life. The national or language parish was an important element in the immigrant community. More than anything else, it represented the continuity of the Old World in the midst of the new.

4) Over a period of three generations, *the immigrants had become extensively assimilated into the culture of the host society,* into its political and social ideals. As citizens they participated as equals in the political processes of the new world. As the immigrants became "middle-class American" they brought the Church with them into the middle-class style of American life. The Church became middle class, but retained its sense of loyalty to Rome and the Holy Father.

5) *The national or language parish proved to be a most important factor in the continuity of the faith of the immigrants.* It provided not only religious continuity; it provided a cultural and language continuity. It was an environment where immigrants were "at home" in the midst of a new and strange world. It did

not prevent the assimilation of the immigrants. Rather it provided the "position of strength" from which the immigrants
moved with confidence into the mainstream of American life. By
the third generation, the usefulness of the national parish had
all but disappeared. As part of the American experience, the
grandchildren of the immigrants had lost the language, had become involved in the political and economic and social activities
of American society, had intermarried with persons of other
ethnic or religious backgrounds, and had moved to the suburbs.
The national parish was left behind to receive other newcomers
who were coming to the United States. Therefore, in a political
and social context such as that of the United States, any fear
that a national or language parish would impede or slow assimilation was unfounded.

Differences still remain. The use of holidays, food, heroes,
and national achievements of the old country are interwoven in
celebration of the ethnic background. But the living substance
of the old culture is gone. The basic values which guide human
life, the social customs and life style represent, in all their variety, the expression of a common culture which is accurately
called the "American way of life." The recollection of the "ethnic
identity" is largely what Herbert Gans calls "symbolic ethnicity."[29]

6) The great fear is that, *in their adjustment to middle-class
American society, Catholics have simply accepted the dominant
values of American life.* These go far beyond the basic constitutional freedoms and liberties. At this moment, they involve an
unrestrained competition for upward social and economic
status and a spirit of consumerism which tends to smother
human life in trivialities and results in the misuse of the resources which should be available to feed the world. An uncertainty and ambiguity has arisen about moral and ethical values,
and the economic and military might of the nation can result in
an arrogance which is destructive internally and externally. As
Herberg says, the prophetic spirit of the Church has been lost in
a tendency to enjoy the benefits of American life while providing
religious supports for the institutions which provide the bene-

fits. This creates an uncomfortable relation of religion to a dominant culture which may constitute a challenge to the Church. A creative and prophetic challenge to the dominant values of the nation may be called for. If that emerges, it will result in a new and possibly revolutionary change in the relation of religion to American culture.

The Struggle for a New "Inculturation" in the United States

At the moment this book is being written, the late months of 1986, the Church is facing the challenge of a new inculturation into the culture of the United States. One of the most important features of this will be the subject of the next chapter, "The Hispanics." Two other features are significant as well: the re-awakening of a prophetic spirit in the challenge to the policies of the American government in the build-up of military power, and the assessment of the American economy in the light of the gospels and Christian values. This latter is the search for a creative expression of the Faith in American culture.

Although the dominant characteristics of American Catholicism reflect to a large extent the values of middle-class American life, there have been numerous evidences in the present generation of strong prophetic witness not only among Catholics but among members of other faiths as well. The presence of Catholics in the peace movement has been widespread and influential. The continuing challenge to the policy of the United States in Central America has taken the form of prophetic witness as well. And ecumenical groups such as Sojourners, Clergy and Laity Concerned, Bread for the World, Pro-Lifers for Survival, Pax Christi, and the Pro-Life Movement are simply a few illustrations of groups of religiously motivated citizens who are raising serious challenges to the policies of the United States, particularly around the arms race, increasing militarism, and U.S. support for governments involved in the violation of human rights; feeding the hungry; and the issue of abortion.

This has been manifested on the institutional level with the publication of the two impressive pastoral letters of the American bishops: *The Challenge of Peace: God's Promise and Our Response*,[30] a judgment about the arms race; and the more recent *Economic Justice for All: Catholic Social Teaching and the U.S. Economy*.[31] The letter on the arms race was a significant event in American Catholicism. It represented for the first time an official statement of the official Catholic Church challenging, on moral grounds, the policies of the U.S. government. The letter was given extraordinary attention and is seen as an important prophetic statement about the religious and moral principles which must guide American public life. The final version of the letter on the U.S. economy has just been published. Although it has not received as much public attention as the letter on war and peace, it is a serious questioning of the U.S. economy in the light of religious and moral values. Although previous statements of the Church, such as the papal encyclicals, have challenged the capitalistic economy in general, this is the first time that American bishops have raised a moral and religious challenge to the functioning of the U.S. economy. They find the continuation of high levels of poverty in this, the wealthiest nation in history, to be a serious condition of injustice that must be corrected. Thus, the strong affirmation has been made that if the spirit of the gospels is to be "inculturated" in American society, some fundamental changes must be made in American policy and in the American way of life.

At the same time, a great deal of thinking is in progress about the institutional changes that inculturation would involve in American society. This has been a continuing effort in the history of the United States. But at the present time it proceeds with a twofold methodology: first, sociological analysis which seeks to identify with the help of the social sciences the structure and functioning of American society; and secondly, theological reflection, which seeks, with the help of scripture and religious traditions, to arrive at a judgment about American society in the light of the gospels. The pastoral letters of the bishops on the arms race and the economy are certainly part of this effort.

At the level of scholarly inquiry, the *Notre Dame Study of American Catholic Parish Life* is another aspect of it. Some years ago, the Jesuits of the United States published *A Context of Our Ministries*,[32] an effort on their part to arrive at a judgment on American culture in the light of the gospels. The Mexican American Cultural Center in San Antonio has its own approach to the problem from the viewpoint of the culture of Hispanic newcomers in the United States. Scholars like Andrew Greeley use sophisticated research methods to provide an accurate description of the Catholic population of the United States. His empirical findings present a surprising picture of American "middle-class" Catholics — still identifying themselves as Catholic although often in disagreement with the Church's teaching; and, in many case, displaying a serious spiritual life with new perceptions of God and religion.[33] Sociologists of religion such as Robert Bellah, Peter Berger, John A. Coleman and others, seek to identify the relationship of religious values to American life. John Coleman's book, *An American Strategic Theology*[34] is one of the most helpful analyses of the entire issue. Calling upon wide resources in his specialized field of sociology, but with an impressive range of historical and theological materials, he describes the present crisis of Catholicism in the United States and outlines the features of a "political theology for the Americas." Coleman locates the crisis of Catholicism in much the same way it has been described in the previous pages of this chapter, namely, the loss of the symbols and practices and solidarities of the immigrant communities and parishes and the rise of Catholics generally to middle-class status. No new symbols, practices, and solidarities have been created to take their place. There has been the general acceptance of the middle-class way of life with its supporting values and ideals; but the recognition has been dawning that these are not authentic fulfillments of genuine Catholic ideals. Furthermore, Coleman thinks that Catholics have lost the sense of mysticism and contemplation in a religious style oriented to action and pragmatic achievements. Yet he insists that Catholic involvement in any society — including America — must be committed to justice as an essential manifestation of faith.

His notes for a political theology, therefore, involve a commitment of the Church to the cause of justice; a realistic awareness of the strengths and limitations of American society; an understanding that Americans must face the sacrifices implicit in the development of the Third World; a grounding of its life in the scriptures, with decidedly religious ideals; a fulfillment in its life of American ideals of freeedom and fairness; and a realization that there are limitations to any political theology, that it must be open to modification and change.

The Coleman model is one of many suggested by the sociological studies and the theological reflection of scholars and religious leaders. They are all part of the widespread effort to create a meaningful cultural expression of the Catholic faith in the United States at the present time. This is a new challenge, very different from that which the Church faced in the immigrant experience in the United States. In a sense, Catholics *are* the United States now in a way they never have been before. This means they should be in a position to give expression to their faith more vigorously than ever before. But there is the other side of the coin: they *are* the very culture they seek to change. As the Jesuits declared in their 32nd General Congregation: "We ourselves share the blindnes and injustice of our age. We ourselves are in need of evangelization."[35] This is a problem American Catholics never faced before. If they face it successfully, a new and creative inculturation will result which will represent a revolutionary relationship of the Church to the emerging world of the United States. While this goes on, one great and visible change is rushing in upon the Church, the coming of the Hispanics. This aspect of the challenge will be examined in the following chapter.

Notes

1. There is an abundant literature on the history of immigration to the United States. The definitive reference work on the subject is the *Harvard Encyclopedia of American Ethnic Groups*, Stephen Thornstrom, Ann Orlov, and Oscar Handlin, eds. (Cambridge, Massachusetts: Harvard University Press, 1980). This has an account of each of the ethnic groups together with topical articles about the many aspects of the study of immigration. There are also very good studies of each of the ethnic groups. In relation to the present chapter, Cecil

Woodham Smith, *The Great Hunger* (New York: Harper and Row, 1963), gives the background to the Irish migration at the time of the famine; William Shannon, *The American Irish* (New York: MacMillan, 1962), is an excellent study of Irish experience and the Irish character in America; Oscar Handlin, *Boston's Immigrants* (Cambridge, Massachusetts; Harvard University Press, rev. ed., 1959), examines the adjustment of the Irish to the Boston area. The background of the Germans is found in Albert B. Faust, *The German Element in the United States*; two volumes, reprint (New York, 1969). Richard O'Connor, *The German Americans* (New York, 1968), described the Germans in the United States; Philip Gleason, *The Conservative Reformers: German-American Catholics and the Social Order* (Notre Dame: Notre Dame University Press, 1968), provides information about the role of the Germans in the Catholic Church. For the Italians, Robert F. Foerster, *The Italian Emigration in Our Time*; reprint (New York, 1968), provides the background of the Italians before they came; Alexander De Conde, *Half Bitter, Half Sweet: An Excursion into Italian-American History* (New York, 1971), provides the history of Italians in the United States; Silvano Tomasi, *Piety and Power: The Role of Italian Parishes in the New York Metropolitan Area, 1830-1930* (Staten Island, NY: Center for Migration Studies), is a study of the Catholic experience of the Italians in New York.

2 Two excellent histories of the Catholic Church in the United States have appeared in recent years: James Hennesey, S.J., *American Catholics: A History of the Roman Catholic Community in the United States* (New York: Oxford 1981); and Jay Dolan, *The American Catholic Experience: A History from Colonial Times to the Present* (New York: Doubleday, 1985). Both have extensive bibliographic notes which are helpful.

3. See William S. Bernard, "History of U.S. Immigration Policy," in the *Harvard Encyclopedia of American Ethnic Groups*.

4. See Joseph P. Fitzpatrick, *Puerto Rican Americans: The Meaning of Migration to the Mainland*, 2nd edition (Englewood Cliffs, N.J.: Prentice-Hall, 1986).

5. See Dolan, *The American Catholic Experience*, Chapter III.

6. *Dignitatis Humanae, Declaration on Religious Freedom, The Documents of Vatican II*, edited by Walter M. Abbott, S.J. (New York: Herder & Herder, 1966), pp. 672-700.

7. Dolan, *The American Catholic Experience*, p. 111.

8. For the political skill of the Irish, see the chapter on "The Irish" in Nathan Glazer and Daniel P. Moynihan, *Beyond the Melting Pot*; 2nd edition (Cambridge, Massachusetts: M.I.T. Press, 1970), and William Shannon, *The American Irish*.

9. See Richard Shaw, *Dagger John: The Unquiet Times of Archbishop John Hughes of New York* (New York: 1977) for the political leadership given to Catholics by Archbishop Hughes.

10. See *Dignitatis Humanae*. Also J. Courtney Murray, S.J., *We Hold These Truths*, (New York: Sheed & Ward 1960).

11. Joseph P. Fitzpatrick, S.J., "The Role of the Parish in the Spiritual Care of Puerto Ricans in the New York Archdiocese," in *Studi Emigrazione*, Centro Studi Emigrazione, Rome, Italy, Ann III, n. 7 (October, 1966) pp. 1-29.

12. See Joseph P. Fitzpatrick, S.J., "Cultural Change or Cultural Continuity: Pluralism and Hispanic Americans," in *Hispanics in New York: Religious, Cultural and Social Experiences*, Office of Pastoral Research, New York Archdiocese, 1011 First Avenue, New York, New York 10022, vol. II, pp. 57-75, for a discussion of the national parishes in relation to assimilation.

13. The definitive work on cultural assimilation in the United States is found in Milton Gordon, *Assimilation in American Life* (New York: Oxford, 1964).

14. One of the best presentations of the basic values of the culture of the United States is found in Robin Williams, *American Society: A Sociological Interpretation*; 3rd edition (New York: Knopf, 1970). See Chapter 11 especially.

15. Daniel Patrick Moynihan, *Family and Nation* (New York: Harcourt Brace Jovanovich, 1986), has an excellent discussion of the problems of American families. Also Gilbert Steiner, *The Futility of Family Policy* (Washington, D.C.: The Brookings Institution, 1981) and Christopher Lasch, *Haven in a Heartless World* (New York: Basic Books, 1977) describe many aspects of the present family crisis. A well-balanced analysis of the issue is found in Birgitte Berger and Peter Berger, *The War Over the Family: Capturing the Middle Ground* (New York, Doubleday Anchor, 1984).

16. The Notre Dame Study of Catholic Parish Life, University of Notre Dame, Notre Dame, Indiana, is an extensive study of "core parishioners" in Catholic parishes of the United States. It issues periodic reports which publicize its findings. It provides a profile of the attitudes and practices of the Catholics they define as "core" Catholics. Hispanic parishes were excluded from the study. Andrew Greeley, *American Catholics Since the Council* (Chicago, Illinois: Thomas More Press, 1985), is an analysis of survey data which includes the entire Catholic population. There are some striking differences in the two studies. On Mass attendance see pp. 54 ff.

17. For the Cahensly issue and related issues about the problem of Americanism, see Hennesey, Chapter XV, "Growing Pains in the Catholic Community," and Dolan, Chapter XI, "Religion and Society."

18. A particular difficulty for Germans arose during World War I, when the United States found itself involved in war against Germany. The charge that they were not loyal to the American cause resulted in widespread harrassment of the German citizens. In the long run, however, it did not affect the welfare of the German immigrants. They became, as German-Americans, a major segment of the creative contribution of the immigrants to American life.

19. Tomasi, *Piety and Power*.

20. See Robert Orsy, *The Madonna of 115th Street: Faith and Community in Italian Harlem, 1880-1956* (New Haven: Yale University Press, 1985).

21. Dolan, p. 302.

22. Walter Elliot, C.S.P., *The Life of Father Hecker* (New York, 1891). *Le Pere Hecker Fondataur des "Paulistes" Americains* (1819-1888) par le Pere Elliot, de la meme Compagnie. Traduit et adopte de l'anglais avec autorizacion de l'aueur. Introduction par Msgr. Ireland. Preface par l'Abbe Felix Klein (Paris, 1897) was the translation that went through seven editions in France and sent Western European Catholics into a long controversy about the Hecker style of American Catholicism as an ideal for the Church.

23. Hennesey, *American Catholics*, p. 203.

24. Pope Leo XIII, *Testem Benevolentiae*, 1899. The encyclical condemned a number of ideas identified as "Americanism." They were similar to the ideas that Hecker and the American liberals preached. It resisted the idea that the Church should adapt itself to a modern age, criticized the "activist" attitudes of American Catholics, was cautious about the appeal to the Holy Spirit: this might minimize the importance of "external" direction, and resisted any idea that the character of the Church in the United States should be any different than it was in Europe. Dolan (p. 316) thinks the encyclical put an end to "Americanism" in the United States. But he is correct in his assertion that the death blow really came with the encyclical of Pius X against Modernism, *Pascendi Dominici Gregis*, 1907. This went beyond the level of cultural changes to the heart of Catholic theology and Christian faith, the charge that adaptation to modern ideas and cultures would imply that the doctrines of the Church admitted of development in new historical contexts. This implied that Jesus did not give a definitive and changeless revelation of eternal truth, but a doctrine subject to change in the course of history. It would take the Church a long time to correct the damage. Almost 60 years later, the spirit of Vatican II was the public commitment of the Church to many of the ideas condemned by Pius X.

25. Hennesey, p. 203.

26. Dolan, pp. 319-20.

27. Will Herberg, *Protestant, Catholic, Jew* (New York: Doubleday, 1955).

28. Herberg, pp. 285-289. See also the concluding exhortation in *Economic Justice for All: Catholic Social Teaching and the U.S. Economy*, A Pastoral Letter of the National Council of Catholic Bishops, 1312 Massachusetts Avenue, N.W., Washington, D.C., 20005, November 1986, par. 358-65.

29. Herbert J. Gans, "Symbolic Ethnicity: The Future of Ethnic Groups and Cultures in America," in *On the Making of Americans: Essays in Honor of David Riesman*, ed. Herbert J. Gans, Nathan Glazer, *et al.* (Philadelphia, Pennsylvania: University of Pennsylvania Press, 1979), pp. 191-220.

30. *The Challenge of Peace: God's Promise and Our Response: A Pastoral Letter on War and Peace*. National Council of Catholic Bishops, 1312 Massachusetts Avenue, N.W., Washington, D.C. 20005, May 3, 1983.

31. *Economic Justice for All*.

32. *The Context of Our Ministries: Working Papers*. Jesuit Conference, 1424 16th Street, N.W., Suite 300, Washington, D.C. 20036, 1981.

33. Greeley, *American Catholics Since the Council*. An interesting summary of the development of Greeley's research and analysis is found in his *Confessions of a Parish Priest* (New York: Simon and Schuster, 1986).

34. John Coleman, *An American Strategic Theology* (Ramsey, New Jersey: Paulist Press, 1982).

35. Documents of the Thirty Second General Congregation of the Society of Jesus, 1974- , Institute of Jesuit Sources, 3700 West Pine Boulevard, Saint Louis, Missouri, 63108, "Our Mission Today: The Service of Faith and the Promotion of Justice," Par. 23.

5
HISPANICS IN THE UNITED STATES

The Current Crisis of Inculturation

The Hispanic population is rapidly becoming the largest minority population of the United States.[1] It will play a significant role in the history of the United States during the next century. More important, from the viewpoint of Catholics, if present trends continue it will become the dominant Catholic population of the nation, surpassing in numbers the Catholics of other ethnic and nationality backgrounds.[2] The Hispanic poplation may well give a particular character to the Catholic Church in the United States during the 21st century, as the Catholic immigrants from Europe gave their particular character to the Church during the present century.

What form is this influence likely to take, and what will the consequences be for the Church, for the Hispanics, and for the United States? This is the problem of a new contact of cultures and a new problem of inculturation for the Church. It is not simply a continuation of the intermingling of Catholic immigrants from Europe and their gradual achievement of a unity as middle-class Catholics. It is a different situation and a different process. The Church now faces a new challenge of inculturation as the United States faces a new process of assimilation.

Hispanics are aware of the experience of European immigrants. As is evident from the previous chapter, most of the descendants of European immigrants have lost the characteristics of the Euopean culture from which they have come and have

125

been absorbed into the dominant culture of the United States. This becomes the preoccupation of Hispanic religious and community leaders: will this happen to them? Will they become part of a homogeneous population of Americans or American Catholics as they lose the characteristics which give them a specific identity as a people and a specific identity as Catholics? Or will they be able to become an influential part of American life while still retaining their own cultural identity? Is this kind of cultural pluralism possible?

The answer depends on the manner in which the Hispanic population relates to the larger society of the United States and to the existing reality of the Catholic Church as a major insititution of that larger U.S. society. In order to understand this, the two following points must be discussed:

1. The experience of Hispanics; similarities to and differences from the experience of earlier Catholic immigrant groups.

2. Significant elements which will affect the experience of Hispanics and their adjustment to the society of the United States.

The Experience of Hispanics

Hispanics come from a culture that has been penetrated by faith, but in a very different way from that of European Catholics or the emerging culture of Catholics in the United States. Their preoccupation with cultural continuity is focused on their Hispanic style of Catholicism.

However, it is not only the background of Hispanic Catholicism that constitutes the challenge. There is another aspect to the challenge, a kind of challenge the Church has never faced before. The advance of the Church to middle-class status in the United States involves complications that go far beyond the problems of cultural pluralism. It is the challenge of social class. The Hispanics are among the poorest population of the United States, while the Church is largely middle class. Since the Hispanics have come largely without their own clergy, the Church finds itself in a situation not only where an American clergy must minister to Catholics of another culture, but as a middle-class clergy they must minister to Hispanics who are largely poor. It is difficult enough to bridge the gap across cultures; it is much more difficult to bridge the gap across social class. These two issues, cultural pluralism and social class, will be described in detail later.

The Pastoral Letter

The definitive statement of the policy of the Church in relation to Hispanics was published in 1983 in a pastoral letter of the bishops of the United States, *The Hispanic Presence: Challenge and Commitment.*[3] The letter describes the present social, cultural, and religious situation of the Hispanics in the United States; it reviews the response of the Church to the presence of Hispanics; it outlines the challenge to the Church in terms of ministry and response to the social, economic, and political needs of the Hispanics; and it makes a firm commitment to make available whatever resources are necessary to enable the Hispanics to become a vital and creative part of the Catholic experience in the United States. The details of this policy will be examined later. One significant feature of the letter is the firm commitment to a policy of cultural pluralism within the dominant culture of the United States and of religious pluralism within the Catholic Church. The present chapter will examine the possibility of this pluralism, namely, whether, given the reality of American society and culture, this will be possible, regardless of the commitment of the Catholic bishops to its achievement.

The pastoral letter also takes up the issue of the poverty of Hispanics. Without stating it as a problem of difference of social class, the letter calls for a "preferential option for the poor" and asks the Church to be a strong advocate for the poor.

The Demographic Dimension

Basically, the challenge of the Hispanic presence is a question of numbers. They are rapidly becoming the majority Catholic population of the United States. Furthermore, Hispanics in the United States constitute a variety of peoples and backgrounds among themselves. Briefly, who are they?

1) *Hispanos*, the name frequently used for the Mexicans who were part of the territory annexed from Mexico in 1848 after the Mexican-American War; 2) *Mexican-Americans*, persons of Mexican background who have come to the United States since the annexation, who are located largely in Texas, New Mexico, *Arizona, and California; 3) Puerto Ricans*, citizens of the United States from the Island of Puerto Rico, located mainly in the northeastern part of the United States with the largest concentration, close to 50 percent, in New York City; 4) *Cubans*, most of whom, largely middle and upper class, came during the 1960s as refugees from the Castro revolution. They are located mainly in Florida, particularly in Miami, which they have transformed into a vigorous Hispanic business area. Large concentrations are also found in the New York and northern New Jersey area. Another group of Cuban refugees came in small boats in the spring of 1980, many of them different in kind from the earlier refugees. They are known as the "Mariel Cubans" from the port from which they left. Many of them are from poorer classes, many are blacks. Among them also were prisoners and mental cases that Castro sent to the United States. They have been resettled in various parts of the country; many of them have returned to Florida. 5) *Dominicans*, large numbers of whom have come from Santo Domingo to New York and the northeastern part of the United States. Many of them are undocumented aliens (the so-called "illegal" immigrants). 6) *Central and South Americans*, many of whom are immigrants, and many of them "illegals," concentrated in the New York area; many are refugees from the revolutions in Central America.

Each of these groups has its own unique history and its own particular "Hispanic" characteristics. An extensive study would be required to provide those historical and cultural details. Persons of *Mexican* background constitute the largest Hispanic group in the United States, about 10.3 million or 60 percent of all Hispanics, according to a 1985 Census Report.[4] They appear to be almost an extension of Mexico, with constant coming and going across the border, although many have been in the United States for generations. *Puerto Rico* became an American possession in 1898 and U.S. citizenship was given to the Puerto Ricans in 1917. Their political status, whether to seek statehood or independence, or to continue with their present constitution as a "Free Associated State" or Commonwealth, is a seriously debated controversy. Their movement back and forth is unrestricted, and, once they establish residence in the Continental United States, they have all the rights of American citizens. The impact of American culture in Puerto Rico has been widespread. Many of them have experienced the pressures toward "Americanization" before they come. The 1985 U.S. Census reported 2,600,000 Puerto Ricans in the Continental United States.

Dominicans have been coming from Santo Domingo to New York and the northeast since 1960. Since they are not reported separately in the census, no one has a reliable estimate of their numbers, but they are numerous in the New York area and their numbers are increasing. An estimated 120,000 were reported in New York City in 1980. They are generally from lower socioeconomic levels in Santo Domingo, are becoming citizens in increasing numbers, and will constitute a significant segment of the Hispanic population in the future. Over 13 percent of Hispanics who were married in New York in 1975 were Dominicans.

Cubans, one million according to the 1985 Census Report, and *Central and South Americans*, 1,700,000, tend to approach middle-class levels. Apart from the Mariel Cubans of 1980, they are white, more highly educated, and their rate of intermarriage with non-Hispanics is very high.

Together with the numbers reported by the census, there are large numbers of Hispanics who are in the United States without documents, the so-called "illegals." It is estimated that there may be three to five milion.

If the 1985 Census figure of 16.9 million Hispanics is taken, they constitute close to 40 percent of the reported Catholic population of the United States. The Immigration Reform and Control Act of 1986 provides for a grant of eventual citizenship to "undocumented" aliens who were in the United States before January 1, 1982, and who meet the conditions of legalization. Furthermore, the largest flow of legal immigrants comes to the United States from the Hispanic world. This will continue. Present legislation provides a maximum of 20,000 visas for legal immigrants to every nation on a first-come, first-served basis, for those who meet the conditions for legal entry. Pressures of poverty and political upheavals provide a "push," and large numbers of relatives and friends are already here to provide assistance to a newcomer. In terms of the future, one other important factor is the youthful age of the Hispanic population, 25 years for all Hispanics in contrast to 31.4 years for the total population. When this youthful population reaches marriageable age, even if they have small families, it will begin to compound the numbers. Close to 28 percent of Hispanic families have five children or more; only about 15 percent of all American families have that number. All indicators describe a youthful population of high potential growth both from high fertility and continued immigration. Meanwhile the birth rate of the non-Hispanic population, including Catholics, has declined to almost zero population growth.

If these trends continue, and there is no reason to believe they will not, the Hispanics will be the dominant Catholic population in the next century. The implications of this for the Church are most important.

The Impact of Cultural Change

The Church had been brought to Hispanic America by conquest. It was imposed on them by a foreign power from abroad that had subdued them, enslaved some of them, destroyed many of their cities, and absorbed them into the Spanish Colonial Empire. The spiritual conquest of the Spanish Colonial Empire was an extraordinary achievement, marked at times by cruelty and at times by great heroism, resulting in a world that was Catholic in its own way.[5] In contrast, the Church had been brought to the

United States by poor immigrants from Europe who came out of traditions of hundreds of years of Catholicism deeply rooted in their cultures and way of life. Furthermore, as indicated in the previous chapter, American Catholics have become largely assimilated into the dominant Anglo-Saxon culture of the United States and, in their social and economic advancement, have brought the Church to the level of a middle-class American institution.

The massive influx of Hispanics in a relatively short time has brought into sudden contact these two vastly different cultures, and in their contact is destined to influence the future of the Church in the United States.

Hispanic Religious Backgrounds

In order to develop this Spanish colonial culture and transfer it to the natives, the Spanish formed the *pueblo*,* or town, and thus created a community. It was a positive principle of colonial policy that persons could not be human unless they were members of a community. Every community was formed in the same way. A plaza was designed which was to be the center of community life, the place where all members of the community could meet, celebrate fiestas, and participate in religious ceremonies. The main building on the plaza was the church; no community could exist unless God was a member of it. Thus, all the members of the *pueblo* were conscious of being members of a community and the community of necessity was Catholic. When Latin Americans say they are *catolicos*, or more commonly, *muy catolicos*, very Catholic, they do not necessarily mean they have been at Mass or the sacraments; they simply mean that they are members of a people, a *pueblo*, which is Catholic. Periodically the *pueblo*, the community, worshipped God in great demonstrations.

In the United States, the *pueblo* in this sense (the community) never worships God. The nation guarantees to the individual

---

*The term *pueblo* is used to mean both the town or city as a place, and the people or population in it.

the right to worship God according to one's conscience. But practice of the faith in the United States is not seen as primarily a community manifestation; it is a matter of personal choice or commitment. To the Hispanic, on the other hand, to be "Catholic" means to belong to a Catholic people. This sense of identity, based on religion, which came to penetrate the life of Hispanics very deeply, was related to a style of Catholicism with which they were familiar — the Catholicism of the *pueblo,* the community of which they were a part.

Two observations are helpful about this style of Catholicism. First, in Latin America, being religious is not perceived, as it is in the United States, primarily in terms of adherence to the organized Church. To be Catholic in the United States means to be affiliated with the Church, to belong to its associations, and to be identified with its structures. In Latin America, the religious practice is marked by the quality of *personalismo,* the pattern of close, intimate personal relationships which is characteristic of Spanish cultures everywhere. Thus individuals perceive their religious life as a network of personal relationships with the saints, the Blessed Virgin, or various manifestations of the Lord. They look on these as *compadres,** as close friends. They pray to the saints, light candles to them, carry them in procession, build shrines to them in the home, make promises to them, and expect them to deliver the favors, help, or protection they need. Just as in human relationships, the Hispanic needs the *padrino,* the patron, or the *compadre,* so the *santo* is the counterpart in the realm of religion. But this personal relationship with the saints takes place quite outside the organized structure of the Church. Indeed, if the organized Church should

---

Compadres are companion parents, as it were, with the natural parents of the child; the man is the *compadre,* the woman is the *comadre.* Sponsors at baptism, for example, become the godparents (*padrinos*) of the child, and the *compadres* of the child's parents. Witnesses at a marriage become *compadres* of the married couple. Sometimes common interest or the intensification of friendship may lead men or women to consider themselves *compadres* or *comadres.* The *compadres* are sometimes relatives, but often they are not. They constitute a network of ritual kinship, as serious and important as that of natural kinship, around a person or a group.

be shut down, the relationship would go on as usual. Hispanics can be very anticlerical toward the hierarchy of the Church without in any way thinking they are departing from the Catholicism which penetrates their lives. It has often been told that, during the Spanish Civil War, men would risk their lives to rescue their *santos* from the Catholic churches which they had just set on fire.

Second, the effort to absorb all the natives into a Spanish colonial culture and a Catholic community was never entirely successful. Remnants of prediscovery religious rites have continued among many of the indigenous peoples, and the African rites were brought by Negro slaves and intermingled with some of the folk practices of the Catholics. The result is a syncretism of cults and practices which is still very much alive in many parts of Latin America, e.g., the *costumbre* of Central America, the *macumba* or *candomble* of Brazil, the *santeria* of Cuba. These practices are often called superstitions by the North American, and elements of superstition are no doubt intermingled with them. But actually they are a mixture, sometimes of pre-Colombian indigenous rites, a variety of Catholic devotions, and an elemental response to the sense of the presence of the sacred in everyday life.[6]

Both of these features of Latin Catholicism — its traditional community character and its personalistic character in devotions to the saints — are very difficult for North Americans to grasp.

Traits of Hispanic Culture

Hispanics come from a world where family loyalty is preeminent, in contrast to the highly competitive culture of the United States which prides itself on, ideally, giving everyone an equal chance to better himself or herself as an individual.[7] Hispanics have a dominant cultural trait of *personalismo*; they relate to persons rather than to organized patterns of behavior efficiently carried out. This reflects itself in their reverence for the saints, their intimacy with heavenly patrons who act as their advocates. They have a sense of the sacred which has been largely lost in the secular culture of the United States. Probably no other characteristic more than *personalismo* affects the relation of Americans in the U.S. to the Hispanics. Institutions in the U.S.A. tend to be very bureaucratic, and interpersonal relations often have a professional or business-like quality. This fails to meet the expectations of the Hispanics and gives them the impression of a cold, impersonal people. If ministry also has this quality, Hispanics will not be attracted. They have a sense of *fatalism, que será, será* (whatever shall be, shall be), a tendency to rely on Divine Providence rather than aggressively drive to dominate the universe as an American would. Relations of men to women among Hispanics are different from those in the United States: the unquestioned authority of the father, the protection of the unmarried girl, the pride in masculine traits as they define them, are characteristically Latin American.

These descriptions indicate that the Spanish colonial experience brought about a distinct culture penetrated by the Catholic faith and which, in turn, became the cultural support of the faith in the history of the nations which came out of that historical background. This was different from the religious experience of people in a world like the United States where the dominant culture influence came from an Anglo-Saxon background.

As the letter of the bishops describes it:[8]

> As with many nationalities with strong Catholic traditions, religion, and culture, faith and life are inseparable for Hispanics. Hispanic Catholicism is an outstanding example of how the Gospel can permeate a culture even to its roots.

When they come to the United States, they face, on the level of everyday living, a clash of cultures which can be upsetting, aggravating, or traumatic. This occurs anywhere when people of different cultures meet. It is particularly acute in the conflict between the highly individualistic and competitive culture of the United States and the personalistic and family-oriented culture of Hispanics. It is also acute in the tension between the Hispanic style of Catholic life and practice, and the American characteristics which exist in the Church in the United States.

As a result, when religious personnel from an Anglo-Saxon background come into contact with Hispanic Catholicism, the meeting of two different styles of Catholicism can be marked by misunderstanding, misinterpretation, and tension. This will affect the role that the Catholic Church will play in relation to the growing number of Hispanic Catholics in the United States. Central to the issue is the fact that Hispanics are calling for a cultural pluralism which would permit the continuation of Hispanic language and culture in the process of their adjustment to the United States.

As the letter of the bishops expressed it:[9]

> The pastoral needs of Hispanic Catholics are indeed great; although their faith is deep and strong, it is being challenged and eroded by steady social pressures to assimilate.

> Respect for culture is rooted in the dignity of people made in God's image. The Church shows its esteem for this dignity by working to ensure that pluralism, not assimilation and uniformity, is the guiding principle in the life of communities in both the ecclesial and secular societies.

Church and Society in Latin America

The letter of the bishops describes Hispanic culture as an experience in which "faith and life are inseparable." That is true. It was true of the indigenous peoples before the time of Christianity in their elemental sense of the sacred. The remarkable achievement of Spanish evangelization was the transfer of this sense of the sacred to Catholic beliefs and Catholic symbols. Life for the indigenous peoples was essentially religious. With the conquest, the religious quality became Christian. No one can experience life in Mexico, for example, without becoming aware of the way the Virgin of Guadalupe penetrates their lives.

However, the structures of society and of the Church perpetuated a two-class society in which the conquistadores and their followers possessed the land, owned the wealth, controlled the power, and subordinated the peasants to a life of oppression and injustice. The Church was identified with the ruling classes, became associated with the wealthy, and was seen as part of a structure of social institutions which were marked by oppression, exploitation, and injustice. The history of these centuries of Hispanic Catholicism would require volumes to record it, a task far beyond the scope of the present book.[10]

In the post World War II period, however, an extraordinary revolution has taken place in the Church in Latin America. The bishops created a continent-wide Conference of Bishops, CELAM (*Conferencia Episcopal Latino-Americana*); a new vitality burst out in the Church in the formation of basic Christian communities (*Communidades de Base*); and a new formulation of theology, called Liberation Theology, was created by Latin American theologians and has had an unprecedented impact on the whole Christian world. These developments all converged in a dramatic way at the second meeting of the conference of bishops which took place at Medellin, Colombia, August 26 to September 6, 1968. The objective of the conference was to examine the implications of the Second Vatican Council for Latin America. The conference was entitled: "The Church in the Present-Day Transformation of Latin America in the Light of the Council." Pope Paul VI in his first visit outside of Rome inaugurated the conference.

The Conference was a turning point in the life of the Church, not only in Latin America, but throughout the Christian world. It described the situation in Latin America as a situation of inhuman oppression and injustice which could not be tolerated by the Christian faith; it committed the Church to a change of social, political, and economic institutions to correct the injustice and violence that were "structured" into the society; and it reversed the historical position of the Church by asserting a "preferential option for the poor." The Church was no longer to identify itself with the wealthy and the powerful; it was to identify itself with the cause of the poor in their demand for a just and human society. The bishops described the reality of Latin America:

> Its agonizing problems mark it with signs of injus-
> tice that wound the Christian Conscience. . . . Latin
> America appears to live beneath the tragic sign of un-
> derdevelopment that not only separates our brothers
> (and sisters) from the enjoyment of material goods,
> but from their proper human fulfillment. In spite of
> the efforts being made, there is the compounding of
> hunger and misery, of illness of a massive nature and
> infant mortality, of illiteracy and marginality, of pro-
> found inequality of income, and tensions between the
> social classes, of outbreaks of violence, and rare par-
> ticipation of the people in decisions affecting the com-
> mon good.

* * * * *

> Our peoples seek their liberation and their
> growth in humanity, through the incorporation and
> participation of everyone in the very conduct of the
> personalizing process. . . . We have seen that our
> most urgent commitment must be to purify our-
> selves, all the members and institutions of the Catho-
> lic Church, in the Spirit of the Gospel.[11]

The third meeting of the Conference of Latin American Bishops took place at Puebla, Mexico, in February 1979. Pope John Paul II journeyed to Mexico, his first journey as Pope outside of Rome, to be present at the conference. It became an internationally significant event. The declarations of Medellin had become controversial in the meantime and the Christian world waited to see if the bishops and the Pope at Puebla would reverse the commitments of the conference at Medellin. It appeared that no reversal took place.

Meanwhile, the commitment of the Church was manifesting itself in powerful demands for justice and liberation throughout

Central and South America. Violent reactions set in; and
priests, sisters, and hundreds of lay men and women, leaders of
the basic Christian communities, were violently killed for supporting the claim of the poor for justice.

Comunidades de Base (Basic Ecclesial Communities)

The reawakening of Catholic life manifested itself primarily
in the grass-roots development of small Christian communities
called Basic Ecclesial Communities (*comunidades de base.*)

These "basic Christian communities" are small neighborhood or family gatherings in which participants read and reflect
on the scriptures, pray together, and seek to fulfill in their relations to one another a sense of a community united in Christ and
seeking to be of service to their neighbors. They are defined in
the Puebla documents as follows:[12]

> As a community, the CEB brings together
> families, adults, and young people, in an intimate in-
> terpersonal relationship grounded in the faith. As an
> ecclesial reality, it is a community of faith, hope, and
> charity. It celebrates the Word of God and takes its
> nourishment from the Eucharist, the culmination of
> all the sacraments. It fleshes out the Word of God in
> life through solidarity and commitment in the new
> commandment of the Lord; and through the service
> of approved coordinators, it makes present and
> operative the mission of the church and its visible
> communion with the legitimate pastors. It is a base-
> level community because it is composed of relatively
> few members as a permanent body, like a cell of the
> larger community. "When they deserve their ecclesial
> designation, they can take charge of their own
> spiritual and human existence in a spirit of fraternal
> solidarity."

Their significance is described by Penny Lernoux:[13]

> The heart and soul of this pastoral activity — the

first prong of the attack — is the Christian grassroots community (*comunidad eclesial de base:* CEB). In 1979 there were some 80,000 communities in Brazil, or twice as many as in 1976. Composed of small groups of neighbors (no more than twenty adults) in impoverished rural villages and urban slums, the communities usually start as a spin-off from the parish church by relieving the hard-pressed priest of such duties as catechism classes. In sharing the responsibilities of the church, community members often begin to share in other neighborhood concerns, such as a health center or a school. Because religious instruction emphasizes Medellin's concern with "liberating education," the Bible is read as a story of liberation. By applying biblical stories to their own situation, community members perceive an essential parallel: if the God of the Bible was on the side of the poor and oppressed back then, God must be on their side, too. This knowledge is the beginning of the end of the colonial inheritance of fatalism. Children do not die because it is God's will; they die because of lack of food and medicine and unhygienic living conditions. In understanding reality, community members want to change their situation, through cooperatives, a shanty-town association, or similar intermediate organizations that enable them to have some voice in their own destiny. In effect, the communities are practicing their own theology of liberation.

Grassroots Christian communities are unlike anything previously attempted in Latin America in three important respects: they are born at the bottom, not imposed by some government agency at the top; their principal characteristic is solidarity (in the communities it is more important to be a brother or sister than a boss); and they have the institutional support of the church, both locally and regionally. (The government's knowledge that the Brazilian

bishops are prepared to put all their influence on the
line to protect the communities, and to call on international opinion if need be, has been a major factor in
their survival.)

If the *comunidades de base* come alive among the Hispanics
in the United States, they could transform the Church here as
they have in Central and South America.

Liberation Theology

What the *comunidades de base* represent in the area of pastoral developments, Liberation Theology represents on the level
of theology. This is so widely publicized and discussed that little
need be said of it by way of detailed description. From the viewpoint of this book, two things are important: it does represent a
model of inculturation of the faith in the presence of the social
reality of Latin America; it may have some relationship to the
experience of Hispanics in the United States.

Briefly, Liberation Theology[14] is a method of theological reflection that seeks to find the meaning of the gospels in the exis-
tential reality in which Latin Americans live. Given the total
cultural, social, economic, and political realities of their lives,
what is the meaning of the gospel in that total lived experience?
What are the implications of the gospel for that total reality?
One obvious implication is, as Medellin emphatically stated it,
that men and women must be liberated from the injustice and
oppression which prevent them from living fully a Christian life.

In their attempt to describe the kinds of social structures
that would enable the poor to fulfill their humanity in the spirit
of the Gospels, some of the liberation theologians have been
criticized for appearing to reflect a Marxist influence in their
theories. This will be argued out extensively by social scientists,
theologians, and ecclesiastics. Whatever direction this discussion may take, what is clear is that the liberation theologians
have made a profound impact on the Church in Latin America
and elsewhere. They have responded creatively in the effort toward a new inculturation of the faith in a land that called itself

Christian while the social reality was a denial of Christian ideals.

Many of the Hispanics coming to the United States have been influenced by Liberation Theology. Many Hispanic residents of the United States have been touched by it. Therefore, although the social reality of the United States is very different from that of Latin America, the awareness of a method of theological reflection such as liberation theology may prepare them to question the values of American culture and seek a more genuine inculturation of the Christian faith.

Hispanic Experience in the United States

Out of this cultural and historical and religious background, the Hispanics come to the United States and face the problem of adjustment to American society and the problem of expressing their faith in this new and strange environment. The process involves the effort to preserve their language and their culture, the theme of the Pastoral letter of the bishops, *The Hispanic Presence.* . . . The process has come to involve another serious problem for the American Church, the problem of social class. The Hispanics are not only a different language and cultural group; they are among the poorest persons in the United States.

Hispanics as the "Poor" of the United States

Bridging the gap between middle class and poor is more difficult than bridging the gap between cultures. In a sense poor people tend to create a cultural style of their own in response to the problems of survival; this is particularly true when the poor are in the presence of a middle-class population.

The pastoral letter takes careful note of the poverty of Hispanics. The Puerto Ricans — and note that they are the only Hispanics who are native-born American citizens — are close to the poorest population of the United States. According to a 1985 Census Report, 42 percent of all Puerto Ricans were living below the poverty level, that level of median family income that the U.S. Government identifies as necessary for a minimally decent human lifestyle. Only 30 percent of American Blacks were living in poverty. For all Hispanics, 25 percent were living below poverty; for non-Hispanics in the nation, the rate was only 11 percent.[15] A recent report of the Census Department[16] measured the economic status of citizens not by annual income, but by the amount of wealth possessed. In this perspective the poverty of Hispanics is more sharply defined. Although median family income for all Hispanics in March 1985 was $18,833, 24 percent or 4.2 million Hispanic households had zero net worth or minus net worth. In other words, they had no resources except their income or were even in debt.

The third draft of the letter of the American bishops on the American economy[17] calls special attention to the poverty of the children: one of every four children in the entire United States is living in poverty; among Blacks it is one in two; among Hispanics it is one in three. The bishops are emphatic about the need to enable these marginalized citizens to become part of the mainstream of American life. They point very clearly to the problem of social class, namely, the vested interest and control of power in the hands of the more affluent citiizens. The bishops emphasize the fact that large numbers of the affluent are Catholics. Most of the Hispanic poor are also Catholics. Bridging the social class gap, therefore, becomes a special challenge to Catholics, particularly in reference to Hispanics.

The Option for Cultural Pluralism:

In its discussion of Hispanics in the United States, the pastoral letter directs its attention more clearly to the continuity of Hispanic culture in a situation of cultural pluralism.

In view of the American immigrant experience, what is the likelihood of Hispanics maintaining the cultural pluralism they propose? It will be helpful to discuss briefly here "assimilation" as it has been experienced historically in the U.S.A. (see Chapter 4) and "assimilation" as this is understood in the Letter of the Bishops. Likewise some explanation of the concept of "cultural pluralism" must be provided.

Assimilation:[18] Sociologically this has been defined as a process whereby newcomers to the United States gradually lose the language and cultural characteristics of their native land and adopt the language together with the dominant cultural characteristics of the new nation. As indicated in Chapter 4, among the immigrants from Europe this was generally a three-generation process. The newcomers created their immigrant communities, establishing their own national and language parishes or religious congregations and carrying over to a large extent many of the characteristics of their native land. By the time their grandchildren became adults, this third generation had lost the language, had advanced socio-economically to middle class status, had adopted many of the characteristics of the dominant American culture, had relocated in many cases to more affluent suburbs, and had become in a real sense part of a middle-class America.

Note that this had begun as an experience of cultural pluralism, an experience similar to what the Hispanics are proposing today. In fact, the dominant theory for the transition of immigrants to American life emphasizes the importance of this initial period of cultural pluralism, the immigrant communities in which many features of old world life were transferred to the new world. As indicated in Chapter 4, it was these immigrant communities that became the source of strength and stability of immigrant life, enabling them to move with confidence into the mainstream of American life. Thus the prevailing theory of immigrant assimilation emphasizes the importance of this period of cultural pluralism that serves as a helpful transition period for newcomers in their adjustment to American life. There should be no difficulty about Hispanics having a similar experience in their transition to American life. It is the continuity of this cultural pluralism through many generations that has not historically occurred.

However, there have always been groups of Americans who displayed a fear and distrust of the immigrants and who wanted the immigrants to adopt the English language and an American style of life as quickly as possible. This movement was called "Americanization,"[19] and it was resisted by the immigrant groups as explained above in Chapter 4. The stronger the effort to get them to surrender their own way of life, the stronger became the effort of immigrant groups to retain it. It is possible that this effort is what the bishops have in mind when they speak of "assimilation." It was the spirit of Americanization that led to the restrictive immigration legislation of 1924.

There is some evidence that this spirit is awakening again in the case of Hispanics, particularly around the issue of language. Citizens of Dade County, Florida, have passed a law forbidding the use of Spanish in public documents; and former Congressman S.I. Hayakawa has founded an organization called "U.S. English," dedicated to supporting a constitutional amendment declaring English to be the official language of the United States and placing severe limitations on the support of bilingualism. A proposition supporting this concept was passed by a vote of three to one in the California elections of November 1986.[20] It is not unlike the reaction against continuing immigration in 1924. The cry at that time was that foreign cultures were a threat to the continuation of American institutions. The same spirit now reawakens around bilingualism as a threat to the dominant culture of the nation. It is understandable why Hispanics and the bishops would resist this kind of pressure. However, it is not clear that this pressure should be called "assimilation."

In contrast to "Americanization," a concept of *cultural pluralism* began to be developed under the influence of Horace M. Kallen.[21] It is the concept of a process in which various cultures would retain over time their specific characteristics and would establish a relation to other ethnic or racial groups in the United States, something like a loose federation of peoples, sharing a common unity as citizens of the United States, retaining their native language while mastering English, and retaining a specific identity of their own. Kallen described it as a mosaic, or using his own analogy, a symphony orchestra where a wide variety of instruments make their own sounds but are integrated into the unity of a beautiful symphony.

The *cultural pluralism* of Hispanics, and the one described in the Letter of the Bishops appears to be similar to the concept of Horace Kallen. Although this cultural pluralism did appear to be a reality in the early years of the life of immigrants in the U.S.A., it did not survive as an abiding feature of American society.

The question remains: what is the likelihood of the Hispanics being able to maintain a cultural pluralism over the generations within the society of the United States, and in view of the reality of immigrant experience?

Assimilation of Hispanics: The most extensive and reliable analysis of the convergence of Hispanic and American cultures is found in a study by A.J. Jaffe, Ruth M. Cullen, and Thomas D. Boswell, *The Changing Demography of Spanish Americans.*[22] Based on the data of the 1970 Census, it shows a consistent pattern of assimilation similar to that of earlier ethnic groups. Using the indicators of language, socio-economic levels, fertility, and intermarriage, Jaffe and his associates found evidence of a trend toward the dominant cultural patterns of the United States: English becomes the language of common usage; socio-economic advancement improves in the second and third generations and with number of years in the United States; fertility declines with education. They conclude their study as follows:

> The Spanish-American groups in the United States . . . have changed and will continue to change in a manner parallelling the general society. . . . With each passing decade, they are being brought closer to the mainstream of social change and economic development of the larger society until eventually there will be a merging . . . in another generation or two they will be almost indistinguishable from the general U.S. population.[23]

The pace at which this convergence is taking place differs for each Hispanic group, and differs within each group. But the evidence of a trend toward convergence is abundant and consistent. The extensive study of the Mexican-Americans by Grebler, Moore, and Guzman[24] found a large and rapidly growing population, surprisingly recent in the United States, segregated in many areas by discrimination, but nevertheless developing a self-awareness and political strength that will push strongly for participation in the mainstream of American life. Cubans, already middle class before coming to the United States, are moving with ease into middle-class status. Their intermarriage rate with non-Hispanics is extremely high,[25] and their fertility patterns are similar to that of the total population of the United States. Puerto Ricans are dispersing widely into smaller cities of the northeast. The second generation now approaches the educational levels of the total population of the United States. There are noticeable socio-economic advances; and, outside of New York City, the rate of intermarriage increases sharply with the second generation.[26] The standard sociological indicators, therefore, lead to the conclusion that the experience of Hispanics will be similar to that of previous immigrant groups.

The Differences: There are striking differences, however, which may result in a distinct Hispanic experience. In the first place, Hispanics come from "next door." Mexico borders on the United States for 2,000 miles, and the Central American nations are accessible by land. The ease and frequency of travel back and forth reinforces an already deeply rooted culture.

The attention given to culture since World War II has cultivated in all peoples an awareness of their native culture and the importance of retaining it. Furthermore, the increasing emphasis on cultural pluralism in the United States has created a climate much more favorable to the retention of a native culture than was ever the case with earlier immigrants. This became very clear in the Immigration Act of 1965.[27] In all discussions of the future political status of Puerto Rico, the question of the retention of their language and their culture is a critical consideration. Grebler and his associates found a strong retention of language among the Mexican-Americans. Despite the findings of Joshua Fishman[28] that there is little evidence that Hispanics will have any more success than earlier immigrants in retaining their language, this growing self awareness and its relationship to language may result in a different response to American society. The strong emphasis by Hispanics on bilingual and bicultural programs in the public schools is only one reflection of this strong sense of culture and a determination to perpetuate it.

However, there are other features of Hispanics which complicate the problem of adjustment to the United States. Puerto Ricans, Dominicans, and the Cubans who arrived in 1980 are a racially mixed population. They range in color from completely Caucasoid to completely Negroid, with all variations in between. Many will be identified as Black in the United States and will face the problems of colored people in American society. Most Mexicans are *mestizo,* the offspring of unions of native Indian populations and Europeans. This is true also for some immigrants or refugees from Central and South America. They may be exposed to forms of racial discrimination which never affected Europeans. All of these details will affect not only the adjustment of Hispanics to American life, but to their life as Catholics as well.

Within recent years there has been an increasing interest on the part of many people to discover their cultural roots, their ethnic background.[29] This may have been stimulated by the emergence of Black consciousness among American Blacks as the Civil Rights and Black Power movements developed. There was a strong effort to find the roots of their identity by searching out their background in Africa. As the emphasis on Black identity found expression in literature, drama, poetry, and art, the Blacks as a people developed an organizational strength that gained many benefits for them as a people and as a distinct group of citizens in the U.S.A. The same may occur among Hispanics.

At the same time, the white populations began to emphasize their own ethnic identity as Irish-Americans, Italian-Americans, Polish-Americans, etc. Ethnic consciousness came to be celebrated and expressed in festivals, neighborhood parties, and in a literature and drama of its own.[30] This awakening of ethnic consciousness has been explained by some social scientists as a white backlash against the growing strength of American Blacks; others explain it as a reaction against the loneliness and *anomie* of contemporary middle class life; others see it as a spontaneous effort to retain what supports for self-identity are still available in a world marked by uncertainty and rapid change.

A Pluralism of Interests

Although the pluralism proposed by Horace Kallen did not continue, scholars point out that a different kind of pluralism did develop, what Milton Gordon calls, "structural pluralism" and what Glazer and Moynihan call "interest groups."[31] The immigrants who were Catholic tended to group together around Catholic interests (whether they were upper, middle, or lower class); Protestants tended to gather around Protestant interests: Jews around Jewish interests, particularly the security of the new nation of Israel. Blacks are described as organized around Black issues. American political life has often been described as a remarkable process of accommodating conflicting interest groups in the nation. Gordon, as well as Glazer and Moynihan, insist that the fundamental interest on which group identity is based in the United States is religion or race. If this theory is a reliable analysis of American society, Hispanics would be expected eventually to identify with the Catholic groups of the nation. This may eventually occur. Hispanics spontaneously identify themselves as Catholic, and the Church has become a prominent advocate for Hispanics on many issues, such as resistance to some features of the immigration legislation of 1986 (opposition to employer sanctions), protection of Central American refugess, support of the United Farm Workers, and many local issues. However, the question still remains: despite their identification as Catholics and with the Catholic Church, will they be able to sustain a distinct Hispanic Catholicism over the years and generations?

Scholars[32] admit that, pragmatically, most newcomers realize that commitment to the nation's language, political ideals, and basic cultural values, and the acceptance and support of American institutions are essential for satisfactory living in the United States. All of them admit that American society is not a monolith. It is a society of extraordinary variety. It is a pluralistic society on the level of less significant values. But the possibility of such pluralism on the level of particular values exists only because of the common commitment to the central values of the dominant culture of the United States.

What then does cultural pluralism mean in this context and how is it likely to affect the experience of Hispanic newcomers?

In the light of Chapter 4 and the previous discussion, a number of reliable statements can be made about cultural pluralism as it has occurred historically.

a) Immigrants coming to the United States from foreign cultures have always sought to gather in what has been described as an "immigrant community," neighborhoods where large numbers of a particular group establish stable residence; where language and food, lifestyle and religion, continue as it was in the old country. This was the source of psycho-social satisfaction and sometimes became the basis of political power. It was the security of this immigrant community that enabled its members to move with self-confidence and strength into the mainstream of American society.

b) By the third and fourth generation, these immigrant communities had gradually disappeared, not because of any pressure or compulsion, but as a result of the spontaneous response of the descendants of immigrants to their experience of American life.

Is Cultural Pluralism for Hispanics a Possibility?

With reference to Hispanics, the question remains to be asked: In the light of the previous experience of immigrants and the experience of Hispanics until now, what is the future likely to hold for Hispanics in terms of the inculturation into the dominant culture of the United States, or in terms of the continuation over generations of their Hispanic language and culture?

Language: No other immigrant group has made the issue of language as serious a political issue as have the Hispanics. They want their language preserved. The Mexican-Americans particularly were successful in having the Bi-Lingual Education Act passed in 1968. The act provides that, "in recognition of the special education needs of the large numbers of children of limited English speaking ability in the United States, Congress hereby declares it to be the policy of the United States to provide financial assistance to local educational agencies to develop and carry out new and imaginative elementary and secondary school programs to meet these special educational needs." Some of the plans suggested in the Senate hearings on the act included: 1) teaching Spanish as the native language; 2) teaching English as a second language; 3) efforts to attract and retain as teachers, promising individuals of Mexican or Puerto Rican descent; and 4) efforts to establish closer cooperation between the school and the home.

Two different concepts of bilingualism were predominant during the hearings.[33] One saw bilingualism as transitional, as a pragmatic program to get students to master English as quickly as possible. The second emphasized that the purpose of bilingualism was not only the mastery of English, but the preservation of Spanish, and hence the development of completely bilingual students. The first orientation prevailed in the statement of the act's objective.

The Bi-Lingual Education Act has no compulsory features; it provides financial assistance in response to proposals submitted by education agencies, public or private. Thus, its application depends on the initiative of local boards of education submitting proposals and, if they are funded, in carrying out the program effectively. It has had a troubled history, constantly under attack from its opponents. Poorly administered in some instances, it has had excellent results in the hands of serious and committed teachers and administrators. The Reagan Administration (1980-onward) has tried consistently to do away with the act, but Congress still continues it. Apart from its academic potentiality or success, it has become a political issue which the Hispanics have always seen as a sign of their political strength.

Apart from the Bi-Lingual Education Act, the Supreme

Court decision in *Lau v. Nichols*[34] asserted that, if children are required to attend school but do not know English well enough to be instructed in English, they have a civil right to be instructed in a language that they understand. Thus, for limited English-speaking persons, bilingual education becomes a civil right enforced by the courts. However, the two major orientations of the Senate hearings on the Bi-Lingual Education Act appeared again around the programs mandated by the courts. It is generally interpreted to require bilingual education only until the student knows English well enough to participate in regular classes. The Hispanics keep insisting that it should be continued to enable the students to retain fluency in Spanish while they master the English language. The determined effort of the Hispanics for bilingualism is a reflection of the strong sense of the importance of cultural continuity by the maintenance of the Spanish language.

One very pragmatic feature of the interest in bilingualism is the fact that Hispanics return so often to their country of origin. This is particularly true of Puerto Ricans, who are native-born citizens of the United States. They travel without restriction between the island and the continent. Many Puerto Rican families return to live in Puerto Rico after living for many years in the continental United States. A study in 1982 found that there were 85,000 Puerto Rican students in the public schools of Puerto Rico who did not know Spanish well enough to be instructed in Spanish.[35] These were students returning after years on the continent. Thus the continuity of Spanish language is essential in view of the possibility of return.

Finally, in a period of history when the interests of the United States are so closely linked to those of Central and South America and the Spanish-speaking Caribbean, the great advantage of a bilingual Spanish/English population is evident.

All of this adds new dimensions to the issue of bilingualism. It is possible that the determined effort of Hispanics may result in a change in language policy in the nation, in the recognition of the importance of preserving the languages of newcomers in-

stead of allowing them to be lost as has been the sad experience
of all previous immigrants to the United States.[36]

The Continuity of Culture as a Support for the Faith

As indicated above, the pastoral letter of the bishops, *The
Hispanic Presence* . . . indicates there has been a deep relationship between Hispanic culture and the Catholic faith. For many
Hispanics, their religion was a cultural event. This is true of all
peoples after the faith has found a deeply rooted expression in
any particular culture. But with Hispanics this adds some special features to their experience as newcomers to American life.
To a large extent, the Hispanics who come to the United States
of America lack the formation in the faith that comes from continued instruction. Nevertheless, as a result of the creative effort of the Spanish colonizers, a remarkable cultural environment supported the faith of the people even in the absence of
clergy or detailed instruction and formation. As a result the
change of religious environment is a more profound shock to
them and the adjustment to a new environment and culture is
much more difficult.

For earlier immigrants, the presence of large numbers of
their own clergy and religious constituted a continuity of culture. This the Hispanics do not enjoy. The Hispanics are the first
Catholic immigrants to come to the United States in large numbers without a native clergy to accompany them. This has
created a great challenge to the clergy of the United States to
minister to a large population of different language, different
cultural background, and different social class. It has resulted
in an equally serious problem for the immigrants. They find a
new and strange religious environment in which it is difficult
for them to feel at home, and where, even in the area of religious
practice, they often suffer from widespread misunderstanding
and prejudice. The response of the American clergy has been admirable even though it has been inadequate.[37] Thousands of
American priests and religious personnel have gone to great
lengths to learn the Spanish language and to familiarize themselves with the background of Hispanic culture to prepare themselves to minister to the newly arriving Hispanics. Sponsored by

Cardinal Spellman and financially supported by him, the Institute of Intercultural Communication was established in Ponce, Puerto Rico, in 1957. During fifteen years it prepared hundreds of priests, religious, and lay personnel in language and culture for ministry to Hispanics, particularly Puerto Ricans.

At a later date the Mexican American Cultural Center (MACC) was established by Father Virgilio Elizondo in San Antonio, Texas. This Center has had a remarkable influence through its preparation of Americans for Hispanic ministry. Controversial though it later became, nevertheless the Center of Intercultural Documentation (CIDOC) established by Ivan Illich in Cuernavaca, Mexico, had a significant influence, not only in language preparation, but in its challenging critique of contemporary cultures and their relationship to the Church. Furthermore, large numbers of priests, sisters, brothers, and lay persons devoted themselves to the apostolate in Central and South America. After years of experience, many of them returned to minister to the Hispanics in the United States. At the heart of all these programs was the firm insistence that ministry to Hispanics must be in their own language and in a style that made sense to them, in which they felt at home. Thousands of priest, religious, and lay people sought to do this. Many did it well. This was never sufficient to meet the growing challenge of the Hispanic presence, but I know of no period in the history of the Church when a host community has gone to the lengths to which the American Church has gone to prepare American Catholics to receive a new population of different language and cultural background. To take one example, in the New York Archdiocese, twenty-nine percent of all parishes have Mass in Spanish every Sunday, in most cases with a priest who has learned the Spanish language and the background of Hispanic culture. In the study of Hispanics in the New York Archdiocese, there was evidence of a favorable response to the ministry of these priests. Hispanics felt welcome and at home among them.

The Reaction of Hispanics to American Life

Hispanics in the United States have been active in their own way in response to American life. Long before the First National

Assembly of Catholics in Detroit in 1976, the "Call to Action," Hispanics had already conducted two national assemblies, *Encuentros,* as they are called. They conducted the *Third Encuentro* in Washington, D.C., in the summer of 1985, a remarkably organized assembly marked by an involvement of grass roots people in a way that is rare among American organizations. At the "Call to Action" Assembly in Detroit in 1976, the Hispanic Caucus was the best organized and possibly the most influential. Hispanic priests have organized into an association called *Padres,* and Hispanic Sisters have an organization called *Las Hermanas.* There is a national organization of Jesuit Priests in Hispanic Ministry and a host of local organizations. Noticeable throughout the nation has been the impact of the *Cursillo* movement, a brief retreat designed to achieve a deep conversion of the individual, that is followed up by regular meetings to keep the conversion alive. The Charismatic Movement is widespread among Hispanics, and the Christian Family Movement (*Movimiento Christiano Familial*) is active and strong. Thus, on their own initiative, there is much evidence that Hispanics are taking their religious life in their own hands and are showing impressive signs of strength.

The Support of the Institutional Church

Most dioceses where Hispanics are numerous have established an Office of Hispanic Ministry, to coordinate the apostolate to Hispanics throughout the diocese. At the national level, the U.S. Catholic Conference has established a secretariat for the Spanish-speaking to represent the interests of Hispanics at the level of the Conference of bishops. Seven Hispanic bishops (as of 1986) have been named as Ordinaries in the nation; nine others are Auxiliaries. Hispanics are not at all satisfied with the response of the Church at the level of the appointment of bishops or at the level of employment in the dioceses which have large Hispanic populations. One of the major commitments made by the bishops in their pastoral *The Hispanic Presence* . . . was the effort to make improvements in the appointment of Hispanics to significant positions in the dioceses and the Church.

Vocations

One of the most serious concerns of the Church is the small number of Hispanic vocations to the priesthood and to religious life. The number of vocations is alarmingly small. In a background paper for the New York study of Hispanics, Father Rutilio del Riego gives the number of 190 seminarians during the year 1981-82.[38] Seventy-eight of these were at the prepseminary, high school level; 66 at the college level; 46 at the level of theology. Vocations to the priesthood were never numerous generally in Latin America; the tradition is not there to build on. Also to be considered is the drop in vocations almost everywhere throughout the world. However, there are signs of change. In Central America, there are more candidates for the Jesuit novitiate than it is prepared to handle. Vocations are increasing as well in Puerto Rico, Mexico, Brazil, and Argentina. One major problem that is widely acknowledged is the fact that the cultural environment of an American seminary is not an atmosphere in which an Hispanic feels at home. Many of the religious communities have begun the practice of having their noviceship, and possibly later training, in one of the Hispanic lands to provide a more favorable cultural setting for the candidates.

The National Parish

In many dioceses Hispanics lack the national or language parish which was the heart of the immigrant community and which gave great stability and an abiding sense of identity to immigrant peoples. More than anything else, this constitutes the differing experience of Hispanics and complicates the role the Church may play in their adjustment to American culture. As indicated earlier,[39] the national or language parish was the heart of the older immigrant communities; it was the basis for an abiding sense of identity providing the stability and security that enabled the European immigrants to move with a sense of self-reliance into the mainstream of American social and political life. The issue of "national parishes" for Hispanics has been a troubled and controversial one.[40] It is related to the lack of a native clergy as well as to the fact that the Hispanics arrived just as the problems of the older national parishes were becoming a heavy burden on American dioceses. A method of pastoral care to fulfill the functions of the older national parishes remains a major challenge to the Hispanic apostolate.

The absence of the national parish is one factor that leaves Hispanics vulnerable to the influence of Pentecostal and storefront churches. The one thing these small communities give is a sense of abiding community, an environment in which Hispanics are "at home" (*en su casa*) among their own.[41] Thus an essential part of Hispanic ministry must be the establishment of an environment, a cultural *ambiente* where Hispanics have the satisfying sense of a continuity of their way of life in a new and strange world. This must be the basic feature of the apostolate. Since this is not provided through the establishment of national Hispanic parishes, other pastoral methods must be found to create a cultural environment which will be a support for the faith of Hispanics while they face the adjustment to American life. This is why *comunidades de base* may be important.

Furthermore, ministry in Spanish and in a style with which the Hispanics are familiar is essential: the continuity of *personalismo,* and the family style of religious practice and the public celebrations, especially the processions, and the respect for many of the popular devotions which have great meaning for Hispanics. This is certainly what the Bishops are emphasizing in their pastoral letter when they caution against what they call "assimilation," an attempt to transfer Hispanic religious practice too quickly to American models.

Over the years, as a result of social and neighborhood changes, many of the older territorial parishes or former national parishes of Germans, Italians, etc., have become entirely Hispanic. A sense of identity develops in these areas and the parish fulfills the function that the earlier national parishes fulfilled. In this sense, they become the basis of a community experience which is essential to the continuity of the faith among a migrating population.

However, strong and stable as it was, the national parish did not succeed in resisting the process of gradual assimilation of the populations into the dominant features of American life. As described in Chapter 4, the grandchildren of immigrants, educated in American schools, voting as American citizens, advancing socially and economically, moving to the suburbs, eventually became part of middle-class America. It will require a strong dedication to cultural continuity to resist the same process among Hispanics.

Hispanic Culture and the Changing American Environment

The culture of the United States is in a state of rapid change. This was a closing theme of Chapter 4. The U.S. culture has always been marked by great variety and difference, but a range of dominant values was always evident. When earlier immigrants came, the United States was an expanding society, experiencing the development of great wealth and power. It was competitive, and a commitment to work and the achievement of success (what is called the Protestant Ethic) was taught as a virtuous quality. The legal and political institutions, the legacy of the Anglo-Saxon influence, were solidly in place and respected. Moreover, a spirit of self reliance was honored and inculcated; there was a general concern for individual freedom; and patriotism and strong family values were enthusiastically supported. At the same time, as every student of American history is aware, there were serious deviations from the national ideals, particularly in the institution of slavery, in forms of racial and religious discrimination, and in exploitation of the weak and helpless. But to "be an American" had some consistency and clarity. It was a powerful influence, and access to its advantages gradually attracted the immigrant populations and their children and grandchildren. As they competed for the benefits of American society, they adopted the values and the life style of the dominant culture. They became American.

This consistency and clarity are no longer there. Instead of an optimistically expanding society, the United States has begun to face the challenge of limits; much of the confidence of

Americans has been shaken by the Vietnam War, by political scandals, and by the awareness that the nation can no longer exert the power over the world that it once could. The youth rebellion of the 1960s, the changing values of family life, the impact of television, and the passive yielding to the attractions of a consumer society — all these have created a climate of uncertainty, ambiguity, and doubt.

This new environment can have a deteriorating impact on immigrants or refugees from economically underdeveloped areas. With modern media it reaches quickly and powerfully into the homes and lives of newcomers. It is difficult for them to escape.

On the other hand, the new environment constitutes an openness to change which was not characteristic of America in previous generations. There is a possibility for new values, a variety of religious expressions, and new patterns of behavior. Thus if people with a deeply rooted culture appear on the scene, if newcomers with a deep commitment to basic values should become active in the United States, there is a possibility of an impact of their commitment in place of doubt, of self confidence in place of ambiguity, of conviction in place of uncertainty. As the Hispanics increase in number and influence, the present state of change in the nation may provide the occasion for their coherence into clearly recognizable groups and a powerful cultural influence.

Indeed, this may be the social condition that permits a new inculturation of the Faith in American society. The problems of the changing American society as described above are the conditions described in the sociological analysis and theological reflection that are prevalent today, especially among religious scholars and writers.[42] The impact of the Moral Majority and the increase of religious cults indicate that people in the United States are seeking a satisfying religious life and that American society is open to new religious ideals. Thus the coming of Hispanics in large numbers with a religious tradition that is basically Christian like that of the United States could have a strong influence on the nation in search of a new cultural expression of its basic religious ideals.

Whether this will happen will depend on the extent to which a sense of solidarity develops among Hispanics, a deep sense of identity as Catholics appears among them, and they emerge as a coherent political, social, and religious presence. This could lead not only to a new inculturation; it could develop into a new and positive form of cultural pluralism in the Hispanic population. However, no clear evidence of such a development has yet appeared. But the potential for it is present. If the drive toward social change that is appearing in Central and South America moves northward with the Hispanic newcomers, this could create a powerful impact on American society.

The Second Generation

When we think of cultural adaptation and continuity of cultures, we generally think of newcomers, persons born in a foreign land who come as strangers to the United States from a different language and cultural backgrond. But that is only part of the situation. Probably half, possibly much more than half of the persons we are concerned about are persons who were born in the United States of foreign parents and who have been brought up in an American environment and have attended American schools. This is the second generation and beyond.

They constitute a challenge distinct from that of their parents, and it is a major part of the Hispanic challenge. According to the 1980 Census, 906,825, or forty-five percent of all Puerto Ricans in the United States had been born here. For persons of Mexican background, it was 74 percent. These are the two largest groups of Hispanics.

The study of Hispanics in the New York Archdiocese indicated that the younger the population, the weaker the Catholic belief and the lower the level of Catholic practice. Widespread pastoral experience also confirms that most Hispanic youth have little or no contact with the Church. Yet, when actually touched, pastoral experience also confirms that the promise of spiritual development, generosity, and courage is also great.

The study of Jaffe *et al.* estimates that 40 percent of all Hispanics born in the United States switch to English as the language in the home. This increases as level of education increases.[43] The second generation faces the classic experience of children of immigrants, being brought up in a home of old world culture while they face the impact of American culture through the school, the streets, and the media. They are immersed in all the problems of adjustment to American life. They are trying to retain Spanish while they master English in a world that is ambiguous about bilingualism.

They constitute, therefore, a cultural group distinct from that of their parents. Not completely Hispanic, not completely American, they struggle for a sense of identity in the presence of the strong pressure of an American style of life. Therefore, a youth apostolate among Hispanics cannot be guided simply by the norms used for their parents. The culture is already in transition.

The major thrust of the apostolate should center on preserving in them a sense of pride and contentment in their own cultural background. This means they should be taught about it in schools, parish organizations and meetings, retreats, etc. A sense of respect for their background should be engendered not only in them, but in their non-Hispanic peers, who will also come to respect and honor the culture from which they come. At the same time, they must be instructed in the characteristics of American culture, especially as it impacts on them as youth. They must come to appreciate the positive values of American life and culture as well as its defects.

The second generation Puerto Ricans are called "Nuyoricans."[44] Some of them are moving fast into the high levels of American culture. In a study done by Lloyd Rogler[45] at the Hispanic Research Center of Fordham University, among a carefully selected population of second generation youth, he found a confident sense of their identity as Puerto Ricans and Americans. They were highly educated, were bilingual, and had reached an occupation and income level that was solidly middle class. However, there is another segment of the population that has dropped out of school, is unemployed, and vulnerable to the impact of drugs and crime. Among the girls, teen-age pregnancy is high, and a pattern of female-headed families is also appearing among the second generation as well as the first. Finally, there is the group that are the working poor, those who vote, who belong to labor unions, who are members of parishes, who constitute a stable element among the Puerto Ricans. Few studies exist about this young population. However, the Nuyorican poets have expressed themselves in a colorful literature which reflects their frustration, their alienation, their lack of hope.

This is an extraordinary and challenging variety of young people for whom a creative ministry must be developed. If the Church loses them, it is in danger of losing the future. Spiritual enrichment, educational preparation, occupational training and opportunity, all must be part of the youth ministry. The challenge is to assist the youth to find security in a cultural manifestation of their faith that will preserve the values of the culture from which they come and enable them to accept the positive values and ideals of American life.

This is a most difficult task of cultural adaptation. But it must be faced with a determination to achieve success. The Pastoral Letter, *The Hispanic Presence. . . .* has a strong passage about the apostolate of youth, by youth. "Committed Hispanic youths grasp with the immediacy of their own experience how to share their Christian vision with their peers through means such as modern and traditional Hispanic music and art."[46] It also emphasizes the importance of *personalismo* and the warmth of *cariño* in approaching the young.

In a true sense, it is the second and subsequent generations which will achieve a new cultural expression of the faith, a dynamic blend of Hispanic and American influence. If this takes place, the Church of the next century could radiate a new life that would have a significant impact on the Church and the nation.

NOTES

1. Data about persons of Spanish origin in the United States are taken from U.S. Bureau of the Census, PC80-51-7, *Persons of Spanish Origin by State, 1980.*

Residents in Puerto Rico are not included in these figures. They are citizens of the United States but are reported separately. The dioceses of Puerto Rico are part of the Conference of Latin American Bishops. Also "Persons of Spanish Origin in the United States, March, 1985" (Advance Report), U.S. Census, *Current Population Reports,* Series P-20, No. 403, Dec. 1985. *The Harvard Encyclopedia of American Ethnic Groups,* (Cambridge: Harvard University Press, 1980) has articles on all the major Hispanic groups in the United States. It now serves as a major source of information about ethnic groups and issues in the United States. The most extensive and penetrating analysis of the Hispanic population in the United States is found in A.J. Jaffe, Ruth M. Cullen, and Thomas D. Boswell, *The Changing Demography of Spanish Americans* (New York: Academic Press, 1980). Although based on 1970 Census data, the analysis still provides the best insight into the characteristics of Hispanics in the United States. For reliable information about Hispanics on the local New York City levels, see Jospeh P. Fitzpatrick and Douglas Gurak, *Hispanic Intermarriage in New York City, 1975* (Hispanic Research Center, Fordham University, Bronx, N.Y. 10458). Data for his study were taken from 1975 marriage records in the Office of the City Clerk.

2. There is no reliable source of the number of Catholics in the United States. The figures commonly used are taken from the *Catholic Directory,* which compiles them from reports submitted by pastors. These are estimates, not reliable counts. Estimates for 1980 report a Catholic population of about fifty million.

3. National Council of Catholic Bishops, *The Hispanic Presence, Challenge and Commitment, A Pastoral Letter on Hispanic Ministry,* Washington, D.C. 20005. U.S. Catholic Conference, 1312 Massachusetts Ave., N.W., December 12, 1983.

4. U.S. Census, "Persons of Spanish Origin . . . March, 1985."

5. The best book on the early religious experience of the Spanish in the new world is Robert Ricard, *The Spiritual Conquest of Mexico,* trans. L.B. Simpson (Berkeley: University of California Press, 1966).

6. For an excellent discussion of "popular religiosity" among the Hispanic peoples of Central and South America and the Caribbean, see Jaime Vidal, "Popular Religions in the Lands of Origin of New York's Hispanic Population," *Hispanics in the New York Archdiocese,* Vol. II. An abundant bibliography is provided. An official response to popular religiosity is found in Conference of Latin American Bishops, "Pastoral Care of the Masses," *The Church in the Present-Day Transformation of Latin America in the Light of the Council* (Aptdo. Aereo 5278, Bogota, D.E. Colombia, South America, 1970), Vol. II, Ch. 6. This was repeated at the Third Conference of the Latin American Bishops at Puebla, Mexico, 1979. See *Puebla and Beyond,* edited by John Eagleson and Philip Sharper, "Evangelization and Peoples' Religiosity" (Maryknoll: Orbis Books, 1979) par. 444 ff.

7. A very good analysis of Hispanic culture is found in John P. Gillin, "Some Signposts for Policy," *Social Change in Latin America Today: Its Implications for United States Policy,* edited by Richard Adams *et al.* (New York: Vantage Books, 1960).

8. *The Hispanic Presence* . . ., pp. 4-5.

9. *Ibid.*

10. There is no single book that would provide a brief and adequate history of

the Catholic Church in Latin America. The literature is overwhelming. Most of it deals with the experience of the various nations in South America.

11. *The Church in the Present Day Transformation in the Light of the Council,* Vol. II, pp. 38-41.

12. *Puebla and Beyond,* Par. 641, p. 212.

13. Penny Lernoux, "The Long Path to Puebla," in *Puebla and Beyond,* p. 19.

14. The basic book on Liberation Theology is that of Gustavo Gutierrez, *A Theology of Liberation* (Maryknoll, New York: Orbis, 1971). One of the most helpful articles for American readers is Segundo Galilea, "The Theology of Liberation," *Lumen Vitae* (Saint Paul, Minnesota), 33:3, (1978). Another good summary article is that of Roger Haight, S.J., "The Suppositions of Liberation Theology," *Thought,* 58:229 (June, 1983). The critical letter of the Vatican, "Instruction on Certain Aspects of the 'Theology of Liberation,'" is found in *Origins,* 14:13 (September 13, 1984). This was followed by another letter: "Instruction on Christian Freedom and Liberation" (March, 1986) published in *Origins* 15:44 (April 17, 1986). This is much more moderate than the 1984 letter and appears to be an acceptance of the basic principles of Liberation Theology. It concludes that there is still a place for "theological reflection on liberation. . . . Cleansed of elements that might adulterate it, with grave consequences for the Faith, this theology of liberation is not only orthodox but necessary." See the article by Alfred Hennelly, *America,* May 24, 1986, pp. 425-28. Meantime, however, a leading theologian of liberation, Father Leonardo Boff, was silenced for a year. (*New York Times,* 6/3/85). This led to an outcry in Brazil and a protest by the Brazilian bishops that resulted in a lifting of the penalty. See the letter of John Paul II to the Brazilian Bishops, *Documentacion Catholique* N. 11 (June 1986) 536-540.

15. Poverty Status of All Families, U.S.A. and Hispanic Families 1984

All Families U.S.A.	12%
Total Spanish Origin	25%
Mexican Origin	24%
Puerto Rican Origin	42%
Cuban Origin	13%
Central or South American	24%
Other Spanish Origin	15%
Total U.S.A. Not of Spanish Origin	11%

U.S. Census, "Persons of Spanish Origin in the United States," Figure 2.

16. "Household Wealth and Asset Ownership: 1984," U.S. Bureau of the Census, P-70, #7.

17. U.S. Catholic Bishops, *Economic Justice For All: Catholic Social Teaching and the U.S. Economy,* Washington, D.C. 20005, U.S. Catholic Conference, 1312 Massachusetts Ave., Chapter 3B, "Poverty."

18. See the article, "Assimilation and Pluralism" in the *Harvard Encyclopedia of American Ethnic Groups.* Also Milton Gordon, *Assimilation in American Life* (New York: Oxford, 1964), the definitive work on the subject.

19. See article "Americanization" in *Harvard Encyclopedia of American Ethnic Groups.*

20. See *New York Times,* 11/26/86 for a summary.

21. See Milton Gordon, *Assimilation . . .,* pp. 141-154.

22. See A.J. Jaffe, Ruth M. Cullen, and Thomas D. Boswell, *The Changing Demography of Spanish Americans,* (New York: Academic Press, 1980).

23. *Ibid.,* p. 22.

24. Leo Grebler, Joan Moore, and Ralph C. Gusman, *The Mexican-American People* (New York: Free Press, 1970).

25. See Joseph P. Fitzpatrick and Douglas Gurak, *Hispanic Intermmarriage in New York City, 1975.*

26. See Joseph P. Fitzpatrick, *Puerto Rican Americans: The Meaning of Migration to the Mainland,* 2nd edition (Englewood Cliffs, N.J.: Prentice-Hall, 1987).

27. The Immigration Act of 1965 did away with all restrictions based on nationality origins. It established the public policy that citizens of all nations and cultures would have equal access to admission to the United States. Each nation, on a first-come, first-served basis can receive up to 20,000 visas per year, depending on the general conditions for gaining a visa to the United States. The process is still complicated but the principle is clear: every culture in the world is equally acceptable to the United States. This was a remarkable repudiation of the policy that excluded many persons simply because their culture was judged to be unacceptable in the United States.

28. See note 36.

29. The most emphatic statement is that of Michael Novak, *The Rise of the Unmeltable Ethnics* (New York: MacMillan, 1971). Novak writes with great indignation in criticism of what he describes as the powerful pressures to give up his ethnic identity and become Anglo-Saxon. The book is a confession of the failure of his ways and a plea to the ethnics to resist assimilation. It is interesting that more recently Novak has associated himself with the American Enterprise Institute, part of the new American Right, and an advocate for mainline American capitalism. On the part of the Blacks, the dramatic impact of Alex Haley, *Roots* (New York: Doubleday, 1976) became a national event and stimulated interest among other citizens in their ethnic background. Andrew Greeley, *Ethnicity in the United States, A Preliminary Reconnaisance* (New York, 1974) is a more general study of the issue from a White point of view. William Petersen, "Concepts of Ethnicity," in the *Harvard Encyclopedia* is also excellent.

30. Herbert J. Gans, "Symbolic Ethnicity; The Future of Ethnic Groups and Cultures in America," *On the Making of Americans: Essays in Honor of David Reisman,* ed. Herbert J. Gans, Nathan Glazer, *et al.* (Philadelphia, Pennsylvania: University of Pennsylvania Press, 1979), pp. 193-220. This is without a doubt one of the most important analyses of the phenomenon of ethnic groups in the United States. It is essential reading for an understanding of the contemporary scene.

31. Nathan Glazer and Daniel Patrick Moynihan, *Beyond the Melting Pot,* (Cambridge, Massachusetts, M.I.T. Press, 1963), "Introduction" to the First Edition.

32. Milton Gordon, *Assimilation in American Life,* Chapter 8.

33. *Bilingual Education,* Hearings, U.S. Senate, Committee on Labor and Public Welfare, Special Committee on Bilingual Education, 90th Congress, 1st session, (Washington, D.C.: U.S. Government Printing Office, May, 1967), Part II (June, 1967).

34. United States Supreme Court, *Lau vs. Nichols,* January 1974.

35. George Kaplan, *Of Teachers, Languages and Training: An Analysis of*

the Inservice Training Needs of Teachers of English and of Teachers of Spanish to Returned Migrants in Puerto Rico: Summary Report (Washington, D.C.: The National Institute of Education, U.S. Department of Health, Education and Welfare, 1982), p. 22.

36. See Joshua Fishman, *Language Loyalty in the United States* (The Hague: Mouton, 1966). See also Joshua Fishman, Robert L. Cooper, and Roxanna Ma, *Bilingualism in the Barrio,* (Bloomington: Indiana University Press, 1971).

37. The history of the apostolate to Hispanics in the New York Archdiocese is presented in Robert Stern, "Evolution of Hispanic Ministry in the New York Archdiocese," *Hispanics in New York: Religious, Cultural and Social Experiences,* Office of Pastoral Research, Archdiocese of New York, 1982, Vol. II. See also Ana Maria Diaz, *The Roman Catholic Archdiocese of New York and the Puerto Rican Migration, 1959-1973: A Sociological and Historical Analysis,* unpublished Ph.D. dissertation, Fordham University, Graduate School of Arts and Sciences, 1983.

38. Rutilio del Riego,"La Promocion Vocacional y La Formacion de Seminaristas Hispanos," *Hispanics in the New York Archdiocese* . . ., Vol. II, 225-283.

39. Chapter IV.

40. The problem of the national or language parish for Hispanics is widely discussed. Hispanics arrived just at the moment when national parishes of former immigrants had created many problems for their dioceses. In the process of urban change, the older populations have gone to other areas, leaving the parish with no congregation. Sometimes two or three national churches exist on a single block from which former immigrant parishioners have moved. For the most part, the third generation no longer speak the language and have also relocated. Bishops are much more hesitant about repeating this for Hispanics. For a discussion of the national parish, cf. Joseph P. Fitzpatrick, *Puerto Rican Americans,* Chapter 8.

41. Renato Poblete and Thomas F. O'Dea, "Anomie and the Quest for Community: The Formation of Sects Among Puerto Ricans in New York," in *The American Catholic Sociological Review,* 21 (Spring, 1960), 18-36.

42. See Chapter 4

43. Jaffe *et al., The Changing Demography* . . ., pp. 38-40.

44. See Fitzpatrick, *The Puerto Rican Americans* . . ., Ch. 13, "The Nuyoricans."

45. Lloyd Rogler and Rosemary Santana Cooney, *Puerto Rican Families in New York City: Intergenerational Processes,* (Maplewood, N.J.: Waterfront Press, 1984).

46. *The Hispanic Presence.* . ., p. 20.

6
RELIGION AND CULTURE:
THEOLOGICAL REFLECTIONS

The previous chapters of this book have been largely descriptive of historical moments which involved a major effort on the part of the Church to relate the life and teachings of Jesus to a variety of cultural situations — Paul and the Gentiles, Cyril and Methodius and the Slavonic Rite, the controversy over the Chinese Rites, the experience of the Church in the United States and its adaptation to the many immigrant cultures which mingled here, the challenge of the Hispanic presence. There were also analyses and theoretical comments where appropriate, and the suggestion of some principles to guide those who minister to persons of another language or culture.

Equally important, if not more important, has been the increasing concern of Church officials and scholars about the theology related to cultural adaptation, what they commonly refer to as "inculturation" — the ways of thinking, feeling, and behaving which give expression in the social interaction of men and women to the life and teachings of Jesus.

What is at stake is orthodoxy. What is essential about the revelation of God to the children of God? What must remain unchanged in the beliefs and practices of the Catholic Church? Has there been some form of natural revelation given to the human family apart from the Hebrew and Christian traditions? To what extent can inculturation take place without endangering the true doctrine and practice of the faith? An adequate discussion of this would require volumes; and volumes already exist in which it is discussed.[1] The purpose of this chapter is to review briefly the main points of the theological discussion and discuss their relationship to the presentation of the previous five chapters. It is little more than an introduction to the theological discussions but may help the reader appreciate the difficulties as they are presented and analyzed by some of the best scholars of the Church at the present time.

Vatican Council II
Gaudium Et Spes (The Church in the Modern World)

The great breakthrough in official statements about the relation of the Catholic Church to cultures occurred at the Second Vatican Council and appears in the constitution on the Church in the Modern World. From the opening address of Pope John XXIII through the council sessions, it was clear that a primary focus of the Council was the relation of the Church to the human family in all its dimensions, in all its achievements and all its failures. Speaking of the followers of Christ, the constitution states: "Nothing genuinely human fails to raise an echo in their hearts." The Church is seen as penetrating the whole of history and society and being penetrated by them. It seeks in the document: ". . . to explain to everyone how it conceives of the presence and activity of the Church in the world of today."

From the point of view of this book, what was important was the fact that the council took up the issue of culture as it is discussed today in the social sciences, stated its own definition of the term, and formally discussed the relation of the Church to cultures. Part II, Chapter II is entitled: "The Proper Development of Culture."

The word "culture" in its general sense indicates all those factors by which man refines and unfolds his manifold spiritual and bodily qualities. It means his effort to bring the world itself under his control by his knowledge and his labor. It includes the fact that, by improving customs and institutions he renders social life more human both within the family and the civic community. Finally it is a feature of culture that throughout the course of time man expresses, communicates, and conserves in his works great spiritual experiences and desires, so that these may be of advantage to the progress of many, even of the whole human family.

Hence it follows that human culture has a historical and social aspect and that the word "culture" often takes on a sociological and ethnological sense. It is in this sense that we speak of a plurality of cultures.

This is an extraordinary beginning. But it does not get to the heart of the problem as it is examined in this book. The document tends to perceive the gospels and the doctrines of the Church as one thing and the social and cultural environment as another. The interrelationship and integration of both is seen as a challenge and a problem. But, for the most part, the document tends to be descriptive about culture. It details the characteristics of contemporary culture — the technological revolution, the communications revolution, the explosion of modern knowledge, and new forms of social and economic organizations. But it tends to see these as a situation (the world) to which the faith must seek to relate itself. And it emphasizes the difficulties in doing so. It never reaches the point of asking how doctrine becomes perceived in different ways in the particular cultural context in which it expresses itself.

The council sees "a more universal form of human culture is developing, one which will promote and express the unity of the human race to the degree that it preserves the particular features of different cultures." But it asks how this is to be "synthesized" with the Catholic faith. And: "Finally, how is the independence which culture claims for itself to be recognized as legitimate without the promotion of a humanism which is merely earth-bound, and even contrary to religion itself." In other words, this appears to represent culture and the faith as two separate units which must be integrated with each other. But inculturation means that faith is perceived in the totality of the culture and the culture is the expression in human behavior of the values of which the faith is a constitutive part. The analogy of the incarnation is used in the analysis of inculturation. But Jesus, as man, was not two separate things, linked together in some way. He was one being — at once divine and human. Thus the Council has come very far, but the last step must be explored: how faith and culture interpenetrate each other in a single human society. What is the nature of this relationship; how does the transcendent character of faith continue; and in what sense can culture be said to enjoy an "independence" of its own?

Evangelization of the Modern World
Synod of Bishops, Third General Assembly
October 26, 1974

In an effort to carry out the concepts which were expressed in Vatican II above, the bishops in their synod of 1974 drew up a brief statement about evangelization. They repeated the fundamental commission of Jesus, "Go teach all Nations," as the primary mission of the Church. They also affirmed the importance of fulfilling that mission to the wide varieties of cultures in the world today.[2]

At the same time we experienced the richness contained in the variety. It expressed itself in our attempts to radicalize the Gospel in its entirety among peoples of differing cultures, promulgating in some way the method of the incarnation which God wishes to use in His work of salvation through Christ. In that way the Good News of the Savior shines forth more effectively.

The bishops were aware of the problems involved in the process of inculturation and the threat it could represent for the integrity of the Faith. But this did not excuse Christians from the responsibility of seeking to bring the gospel to the peoples of the world.

The analogy between inculturation and incarnation reflects an awareness of the problem, a process whereby the faith completely interpenetrates the culture as the yeast becomes one with the dough in the unity of the bread, as the humanity and divinity of Jesus were not two separate entities linked together but rather one person, divine and human, Jesus, the individual. The problem, therefore, is this: if the faith interpenetrates culture A, how does it also penetrate culture B, without becoming divided, differentiated, and losing the unity which Jesus proclaimed and for which He prayed: "That all may be one, Father, as you and I are one."

Evangelization in the Modern World
(Evangelii Nuntiandi)
Apostolic Exhortation of Pope Paul VI, December 8, 1976
Latin Text, *L'Osservatore Romano,* December 19, 1975
English Text, *The Pope Speaks* (paragraph numbers are given with citations)

Following the Third Synod of Bishops, Pope Paul VI issued a long and detailed exhortation about evangelization in which he addressed the issue of cultural adaptation more extensively than it had been discussed in Vatican II. The statement is inspired by the orientation of Vatican II, a commitment to bring the Church into a vital relationship with the contemporary world. It sees the mission of the Church as a mission to bring the salvation of Jesus to all men and women, "to present that patrimony to our contemporaries in ways which are as intelligible and persuasive as we can make them." (3) It is "Jesus," — His life, His teaching, His salvation — that we preach and seek to bring to others. But the caution is clearly stated: "The gospel message is unique and nothing can replace it. It will brook neither indifference nor admixture with the principles of other religions nor any kind of compromise, for on it the very salvation of men depends." (5)

Paul VI gives his definition, saying: "that the Church evangelizes when she strives, solely by the divine power of the message she proclaims, to transform the hearts of each and every man, along with their activities, their lives and their whole environment." (18) He then presents what is tantamount to a definition of inculturation: "(The Church) wishes to touch

and transform, by the gospel's power, all the standards of judgment, the reigning values, the interests, the patterns of thinking, the motives and ideals of mankind which are now in disac-
cord with God's Word and His plan of salvation." (19) This is a
remarkable, all-embracing statement. Paul is actually saying
that the gospel must permeate every aspect of the lives of men
and women, so that everything they do and say, and the institutions which constitute their social life must be such that they express the spirit of the gospel. As a social scientist would say: the
gospel must be *institutionalized*. This brings Paul VI to the
heart of the issue of the relation of the Faith to cultures.

> We can put all this in other words and say that we
> must evangelize (not from outside, as though that
> were a matter of adding an ornament or a coat of
> paint, but from within, at the core and root of life), or
> imbue with the Gospel, the cultures and culture of
> man, in the very broad and rich sense these terms
> have in the Pastoral Constitution on the Church in
> the World Today. (20)

If we reflect on the presentation of culture in Chapter 2, the
problem involved in the "inculturation" of faith becomes clear. If
the Gospel is inculturated in culture "A", and also in a different
culture "B", how is this to be done without endangering the essential unity of the Church? The Pope recognizes the problem
clearly and he is solidly in conformity with the revelation God
gave to Peter (Acts 10).

> The gospel, and therefore evangelization as well,
> *cannot be identified with any particular culture but it
> is independent of all cultures.* (Italics mine.) On the
> other hand, the reign of God which the gospel pro-
> claims takes concrete form in the lives of men who are
> profoundly shaped by their particular culture. It is
> also a fact that elements of man's culture and cul-
> tures must be used in building the Kingdom of God.
> Therefore, although the gospel and evangelization do

not properly belong to any culture, neither are they
incompatible with any. On the contrary they can
enter into all of them without being subservient to
any. (20)

This is a remarkably accurate statement of the revelation God
gave to Peter, as Peter expressed it: "God has been showing me
that He is no respecter of any particular race (or culture as we
would say); He accepts anyone of any race or nation who seeks
God and does what piety demands." (Acts 10:34-35.) The Church
was to be "*kat'olos*", Catholic, capable of expressing itself within
the framework of any culture in which men and women sought
God and did what piety demands. However, as was evident in
Chapters 1 and 2, this was not the end, but the beginning of the
problem that has troubled the Church throughout its history.
How do you inculturate the Faith without entrapping it within
the limits of one particular culture?

Paul VI comments: "The separation between the gospel and
culture is undoubtedly a sad fact of our age as it has been of
others." The Church must "make every effort to evangelize
man's culture, or, more accurately, his cultures. These must
achieve rebirth through encounter with the Good News. This encounter will not take place, however, unless the Good News is
preached." (20)

The problem that remains within the context of Pope Paul
VI's exhortation, and for which he gives no guidelines, is how to
determine which elements of a culture are capable of giving expression to the Good News and which are not; what elements
must be present in a culture so that it becomes a suitable expression of the Good News? For example, how were the Jewish
Christians such as Peter to be able to judge that Romans could
live according to the Good News without observing the Mosaic
Law? Even after the revelation to Peter, the Jewish Christians
remained divided about the issue, and seriously divided. What
a difference it would have made if the leaders of the Church in
the seventeenth century saw the burial customs of the Chinese
in the same way they were seen by the leaders of the Church in
the twentieth century! What a difference it would have made in

the United States if the thought and behavior of American Catholics had been judged by Pius X as favorably as they came to be judged by John XXIII!

In discussing the content of evangelization, the Pope returns to the problem of faith and culture. He emphasizes that ". . . there is also an essential content, a vital substance which cannot change or be passed over in silence without distorting the very nature of evangelization," (25) and he lists some of the essentials of the Christian Faith. Then he returns to the important question:

> Evangelization cannot be complete, however, unless account is taken of the reciprocal links between the gospel and the concrete personal and social life of man. For this reason evangelization requires a message which is explicit, adapted to varying situations, and constantly related to the rights and obligations of each individual, to family life without which the development of the individual becomes extremely difficult, to common life in society, to international life and to peace, justice, and development. Finally, it must be a message, especially strong and pointed today, of liberation. (29)

What Pius VI is discussing in this paragraph is the institutionalization of the Gospel, namely the development of ways of thinking, believing, feeling, and behaving, expected forms of behavior which enable men and women to fulfill in their lives the spirit of the Good News. But can a form of marriage in which husband and wife are equal be as suitable a cultural expression of the gospel as a form of marriage in which the husband is the authority? Can the isolation of the aged in American society be related to the Gospel as much as a culture in which elderly people are the most respected and cherished members of a society? If we reflect on the question of culture as described in Chapter 2, the complications of institutionalization become clear. What is the *meaning* that a pattern of behavior has for the persons involved in it? For centuries among early Christians, participation in military activity was seen as contrary to the gospel. Then Augustine developed a theory of the just war. Conscientious objection was frowned upon by the Church for many years; it is now proposed as a legitimately chosen form of behavior for Christians. As Vatican II and Paul VI emphasize, the cultures of men and women change. What is an appropriate form of behavior in the spirit of the gospels in one generation may be contrary to the gospels in another. Even slavery was accepted as a legitimate form of Christian behavior for many years, a fact that appears as a scandal to the Christians of the present generation. The strong position the Pope takes on the liberation of Third World peoples, and the need to eliminate unjust forms of "economic and cultural neocolonialism" (30) is an extraordinary identification of specific patterns of culture which are contrary to the gospel.

What happens is that emerging forms of social institutions, cultural innovations, new technologies, natural disasters (drought for example, or earthquake), the emergence of new ideas, education, communication, as Vatican II describes them, create new situations. The meaning of these must be carefully discerned, and their relation to the gospel profoundly explored. It may take a period of painful disagreement and controversy before a particular pattern of culture comes to be seen clearly as a suitable expression of the gospel. "Not every concept of liberation is necessarily consistent with the gospel vision of man, things, and events." (34) "(The Church) knows, however, that even the most perfect structures and the most ideal systems quickly become inhuman unless those who live in or control these structures are converted in heart and mind." (36) Paul VI never raises the question of war, but his apparently absolute rejection of violence implies a rejection of war. In his address before the United Nations in 1965, his strong words, "No more war, war never again!" also suggests this. His discussion of Faith and cultures closes with a clear and unambiguous statement: ". . . methods of evangelization change according to circumstances of time, place, and culture. Thus they challenge our capacity to find and adapt new ones." (40)

One effort of the Church to struggle with new forms of piety is described by Paul VI in his discussion of "popular piety," what is often referred to as "popular religiosity." What many missioners tried to suppress or eliminate from the lives of the people they evangelized, has come to be recognized more widely today as a fertile, natural soil for the reception of the Gospel.

Both in areas where the Church has been established for centuries and in areas where it is now being implanted, we find among the people special customs expressing their faith and their quest for God. *These customs were long regarded as an adulteration and were even scorned,* but today our contemporaries are almost everywhere rediscovering them and *seeing them in a new light.* At the recent synod, the bishops strove to gain a deeper understanding of them; in this *they showed remarkable pastoral realism and zeal.* (48) (Italics mine.)

One can only think of Bernardino Sahagun chuckling in the Heavens. Sahagun, the great Franciscan, spent the whole of his missionary life in Mexico studying in a painstaking way the religious beliefs and practices of the Aztecs; he spent days and weeks conversing with the Aztec priests, seeking to learn the *meaning* of their beliefs and practices. He also conducted training sessions for new missionaries coming to Mexico. In 1562, however, the Inquisitors visited Mexico, impounded all of Sahagun's writings, and forbade him not only to teach, but to conduct any further study of these "pagan" rites. Fortunately, Sahagun's books were discovered in 1832; new editions and translations have been published, and we now have what the scholarly world acknowledges to be the finest studies ever made on the "popular religiosity" of the Aztecs.[3]

This recent "rediscovery" of the value of popular religiosity is one of the most remarkable examples of the adaptation of the Faith to cultures, the recognition that, when the *meaning* of strange beliefs and practices is profoundly explored, many of them are seen as the natural response of men and women to the awareness of God. Thus, even granting the dangers of syncretism, popular religiosity in many of its forms is seen as a cultural form in which the faith in Jesus can be given a rich expression. The description of the values of popular religiosity in paragraph 48 of the exhortation is an unusually enthusiastic endorsement of them as cultural styles eminently suited to receive the Gospel. The Pope emphasizes as well the need for careful discernment to distinguish between the forms of popular religiosity which are receptive of the faith and those which might corrupt it. The question of "seeing things in a new light" comes back once again — the power of discernment guided by the Holy Spirit, and the gradual emergence of the necessary consensus that a particular cultural pattern is a suitable form of social behavior in which the faith can be expressed.

With all its remarkable insights into the relation of faith and culture, however, the exhortation tends to present them as two separate things that in some way become integrated one with the other. It is not like "adding an ornament or a coat of paint" as Paul VI explains it: it is to penetrate the totality of the culture. That is true, but once institutionalized, the faith *becomes* the culture; faith is given a particular cultural expression. The culture affects the faith as well as the faith affecting the culture. This is where the difficulties arise which are not carefully explored in the exhortation. This is what leads to the troubling phenomenon that believers tend to identify the faith with its cultural expression. The Africans have continually complained that the European missionaries, thinking sincerely that they were bringing the true faith to the Africans, were in actuality bringing them European culture in which the Faith had been given expression for many centuries. The Europeans had lost the ability to communicate the Faith without its European cultural manifestation. A similar problem has marked many of the sincere evangelizing efforts of North Americans in their effort to evangelize the people of Central and South America. North Americans must always be cautioned about a tendency to think that Central or South Americans must become like North Americans in order to be good Catholics.

Paul VI is aware of the problem, and he states it in varying forms, but he never gets to the heart of it. For example, when he takes up the question of local churches and languages (62-64) he cautions against:

> . . . thinking of the Church as a sum-total or a kind of more or less irregular federation of local churches which are essentially different from each other. Rather, according to the Lord's will, the same church that is universal in vocation and mission acquires a varying outward appearance when she sinks roots in varying cultural, social, and human terrains. (62)

It is not the varying outward appearance that causes the problem, but the *roots that the church sinks*. Outward appearances can be easily managed. It is the profound interpenetration of faith and culture that leads believers to think their cultural manifestation of the Faith is actually the Faith itself. *For me it is*. But the task remains to evangelize in such a way that the Faith manifests itself in the culture of the evangelized in a way analogous to the way it manifested itself in the culture of the evangelizers. Notwithstanding the deep cultural differences, the unity of all in the same Faith of Jesus, the universality of the Church must continue to be the sign of the true presence of the Lord. This has been the abiding problem of unity in diversity, of a common identity in the presence of varied inculturations. The Pope continues:

> These Churches must assimilate the substance of the gospel message and then, without in any way changing the basic truth of that message, put it into the language which these men can then understand, and preach it to them. . . . The term "language" is to be understood here as referring to the anthropological and cultural dimension rather than the semantic and literary. (63)

We can recall here the problem of Saint Francis Xavier in trying to find an appropriate term that would convey his concept of God to the Japanese. He discovered after many months that his Japanese interpreter had given him the wrong term. Part of the controversy over the Chinese Rites related to the terms that Matteo Ricci had adopted to communicate to Chinese his concept of God. And today, with the remarkable advances in the sociology of knowledge, we understand the complexities of communicating our concept not only of God, but of the world and science, to persons of a culture different from our own.

Paul VI then gives what is really a summary of the entire discussion in a remarkably clear statement of the problem:

> On the one hand, evangelization loses much of its power and effectiveness if it does not take into account those to whom it is directed by using their language, symbols, and images, answering their questions and dealing with their real lives. On the other hand evangelization risks losing its very substance and entirely disappearing if it trivializes or denatures its content by the way it expresses it or if, in the interests of adapting the universal truth to a particular situation it throws the truth away and breaks the unity upon which the universality depends. Only a Church which remains conscious of her universality and effectively proves herself universal can have a message which is intelligible to all and not confined within local boundaries.
>
> A proper attention to the local Churches can only enrich the Church. Such attention is necessary and urgent for it corresponds to the deep-rooted desire of peoples and human communities to explore ever more fully their own special character. (63)
>
> . . . They suffer deeply when, in the name of theories they do not understand, they are imprisoned within a Church which lacks this universality and becomes regional with no eye to broader horizons. . . . Whenever one or other local Church . . . cuts itself

off from the universal Church and from its own visible center of life, it can hardly, if at all, avoid two
equally serious dangers. One is the danger of secession. . . . The other danger is that of losing its freedom when . . . it is left alone and falls prey to manifold powers that seek to enslave and exploit it. (64)

In Part V of the exhortation, Paul VI describes the persons to
which evangelization must be directed. He incorporates here a
brief description of what he considers the fundamental flaws of
many contemporary cultures, namely, disbelief, atheism, and
secularism. He is very careful to distinguish secularism, "a con-
ception of the world as self-explanatory, so that there is no need
to have recourse to God who becomes superfluous and an en-
cumbrance." (55) He carefully distinguishes this from what Vatican II defined as "secularization," namely, "the effort, just and
legitimate in itself, and certainly not opposed to faith and religion — to discover in all things and events of the universe the
laws that rule them in autonomous fashion, even while the mind
is deeply convinced that the Creator has established these very
laws themselves." (55)

This document is without doubt the most detailed and careful official statement of the Church about the issue of the Faith
and cultures. It reaffirms the revelation given by God to Peter
(Acts 10) that God has no favorites among the cultures of the
world; He accepts anyone of any race or nation (culture) who
seeks him and does what piety demands. The Faith was not to
be identified with a particular culture as was the case with the
Hebrews. It was to be "Catholic," capable of manifesting itself
within the context of any culture whose people sought God and
did what piety demanded. This expression within a culture is
not to be a superficial tacking-on of the Faith "like a coat of
paint" or an ornament. It was to penetrate the totality of the culture, its language, its symbols, its culture. In doing so, it must
not lose the universality of the Faith, but must be an expression
of the essence of the faith in a particular cultural style, thus a-
voiding secession or helpless isolation, but conscious of the unity

it shares with the variety of other cultural manifestations of the Faith.

The varieties of "Catholic" cultures throughout history show that this is possible. Indeed it has been one of the "marks" of the Church, its catholicity. Two problems remain: 1) the tendency of Catholics of any particular culture to identify the Faith with their particular cultural manifestation of it, a kind of religious ethnocentrism. In evangelization, this is the danger, so often found in Catholic missionary efforts, of giving the impression that the evangelized must accept our cultural ways in order to be able to live according to the true faith. 2) The problem, in the evangelization of non-Christian peoples, of determining what cultural patterns are compatible with Catholic belief and practice. "He accepts all who seek Him and do what piety demands." But what does piety demand? Are there features of a culture of persons being evangelized that could not be tolerated; what are the cultural traits, strange and difficult to understand as they may seem, which may prove to be capable of giving a vital expression to the Faith? These are the abiding problems of the Faith and cultures.

The Scholarly Discussion

The official Church has not been the only one examining the issue of inculturation. It is a major point of discussion among theologians, missionaries, and religious leaders. The discussion is directed not only to the problem of the Church in nations that have not been Christian or Catholic; it is directed with equal concern to the problem of the inculturation of the Faith in the nations that have been predominantly Christian or Catholic. This is prompted by the awareness that modern societies which have been deeply influenced by Christian faith no longer give expression to Christian values in their modern institutions. A spirit, called "secularism" in the exhortation of Paul VI, is described as a dominant influence of modern societies, a spirit that sees little need for faith or religious practice. However, the question of justice as an essential constituent of faith has also come into prominence as a major concern of religious persons today.

They have become aware of the scandal, particularly in sup-
posedly Christian lands, of the oppression, injustice, and violence by which the poor are exploited for the benefit of the
affluent. What has come to be known as a "preferential option
for the poor" is an attempt to state the response the Church and
the faithful must make to a human condition that cannot be tolerated among peoples who claim to be followers of Christ. Therefore, the discussion of inculturation has three dimensions: 1) the
inculturation of the Faith in societies which have not been
Christian; 2) a revitalization of the Faith among Christian
people by a new inculturation of the faith in the institutions of
modern societies; and 3) related to both the above, a particular
perception of the problem of justice which must result when the
spirit of the Faith is given expression in modern societies where
injustice is present.

In the following pages some of the major publications in
these discussions will be reviewed briefly, with some comments
added about their relevance for the theme of the present book.

The Promotion of Justice as a Form of Inculturation

Three important events followed the Second Vatican Council
which called attention in a dramatic way to the issue of justice
as a constituent element of faith, and that resulted in emphatic
statements about the need to make faith a vital force for the cor-
rection of instutionalized injustice. The term "inculturation"
was not always used in the statements, but the process that was
demanded meant the same thing.

As described in Chapter 5, in 1968 at Medellin, Colombia,
South America, the Second Conference of the Latin American
bishops took place. The conclusion and documents of the Medellin meeting as presented briefly above amounted to a revolution
in Catholic thinking about faith and justice in Latin America.
"We are at the beginning of a new historic epoch in our continent." The bishops concluded: "It is filled with hope of total
emancipation — liberation from all servitude — personal
maturity and collective integration. We see the painful gesta-
tion of a new civilization."[4]

In a statement that expresses the need for a new inculturation of the faith, the bishops conclude: "We have seen that our
most urgent commitment must be to purify ourselves, all of the
members and institutions of the Catholic Church, in the spirit
of the gospel. It is necessary to end the separation between faith
and life, '. . . because in Christ Jesus . . . only faith working
through love prevails.' "[5] (Gal. 5:6).

To reintegrate faith and life — this is the process of inculturation. In Latin America the bishops see this as demanding a
preferential concern for the poor:

> A deafening cry pours from the throats of millions
> of men (and women) asking their pastors for a libera-
> tion that reaches them from nowhere else. "Now you
> are listening to us in silence, but we hear the shout
> that arises from your suffering," the Pope told the
> *campesinos* of Colombia.[6]

* * * * *

> The Lord's distinct commandment to "evangelize
> the poor," ought to bring us to a distribution of re-
> sources and apostolic personnel that effectively gives
> preference to the poorest and most needy sectors and
> to those segregated for any cause whatsover, . . .[7]

The statements of Medellin became a new cry for reform
throughout Latin America but were reflected also in many other
parts of the world. Injustice and violence were built into the
structures of Latin American societies; it was the insistence of
the bishops at Medellin that this had to be corrected by having
the spirit of faith "inculturated" into structures which would lib-
erate, not oppress.

Justice in the World[8]
Synod of Bishops, Second General Assembly
November 30, 1971 (paragraph numbers directly after quotes)

As a follow-up of the Second Vatican Council, the Synod of
Bishops was a significant event. The document of the Second As-

sembly, *Justice in the World,* is one of the strongest statements made by the assembled bishops of the world (not just Latin America) about the relationship of the Faith to the question of justice. Their statement of this relationship has become one of the classic statements in the discussion:

> Action on behalf of justice and participation in the transformation of the world fully appear to us as a *constitutive dimension* of the preaching of the gospel, or, in other words, the Church's mission for the redemption of the human race and its liberation from every oppressive situation. (#6) (italics mine)

The language of the Synod is couched in the style of social action rather than inculturation. But the consequences of the social action are perceived as an involvement of Faith in the totality of social institutions. The statement is specific about such urgent issues as the arms race, world hunger, oppression and exploitation, refugees, and the rights of developing nations. But this basic theme recurs frequently in the message:

> The mission of preaching the Gospel dictates at the present time that we should dedicate ourselves to the liberation of man (and woman) even in his present existence in this world. For unless the Christian message of love and justice shows its effectiveness through action in the cause of justice in the world, it will only with difficulty gain credibility with the men of our times. (35)

> At the same time that it proclaims the Gospel of the Lord, its Redeemer and Savior, the Church calls on all, especially the poor, the oppressed, and the afflicted, to cooperate with God to bring about liberation from every sin and to build a world which will reach the fullness of creation when it becomes the world of man for man. (77)

Certainly a world motivated by the love which Jesus taught

us, a world of Christians in the service of others, would be a world permeated by the spirit of Faith, a world in which Faith is inculturated.

A Jesuit Response to the Challenge:
31st General Congregation of the Society of Jesus (1965-66)
and the 32nd General Congregation of the Society of Jesus (1974-75)[9]

These were the two General Congregations of the Society of Jesus following the Second Vatican Council. It was in these Congregations that the Society addressed the issues of bringing the Church and the Society into a dynamic relationship with the modern world. Among these issues, one important one was the issue of inculturation.

The 31st General Congregation had the primary responsibility of electing the new General of the Society, Father Pedro Arrupe. It also addressed important tasks of reorganizing the governing structure of the Society in relation to the Second Vatican Council. The concept of cultural adaptation is briefly mentioned: namely, "All Jesuits therefore who work among other peoples should not only treat individual persons with charity and the positive elements of their religion with reverence but in everything which does not run counter to Christian faith and sensibility. They should highly esteem the culture, customs and traditions of these peoples." (426) It emphasizes again the need for those Jesuits working in a foreign land to prepare themselves with a sufficient knowledge of the language, history, culture and religion of the people. (433)

As is evident, the statement in General Congregation 31 is a general statement of respect for different cultures; however, it does not penetrate to the deeper issues of inculturation which were to be addressed in much more detail in later documents of the Society.

However, it was at the 32nd General Congregation that the issue of justice in the world as an essential component of faith became emphasized. The Congregation, like the bishops of Medellin and at the synod, was aware of the fact that the presence of the Church in many parts of the Christian World had not corrected the problems of injustice, exploitation and violence that held many Christians in a form of bondage in societies where injustice and violence were seen to be built into the institutions of those societies. For many years the Society had been addressing itself to the issue of social justice. An important letter, *Instruction on the Social Apostolate* had been issued by Fr. John Baptist Janssens on October 10, 1949[10] in which he urged Jesuits throughout the world to devote themselves aggressively to the issue of social justice, especially in the Third World. The 31st General Congregation continued this emphasis and they began to define it in much more contemporary terms. For example, ". . .And people today are not troubled only by particular questions, for example, about wages, or working conditions, about family and social security. They are especially concerned with the massive world-wide problems of malnutrition, illiteracy, under-development, over population. Thus it is that social action looks more and more to the development of economic and social programs that will be more human."[11]

However, it was in the 32nd General Congregation that the issue of justice as an essential component of faith became a central point of discussion and decision.

> There are millions of men and women in our world who are suffering from poverty, disease, and hunger brought about by the unjust distribution of wealth and resources and by racial, social, and political discrimination. Not only the quality of life, but life itself, is under constant threat. It is becoming more and more clear that despite the opportunities offered by an ever more serviceable technology, men (and women) are simply not willing to pay the price of a more just and humane society. (Decree 4, #20)

The Decree then adds a very significant statement:

> The expectations of our contemporaries — and their problems — are ours as well. *We ourselves share*

> *in the blindness and injustice of our age. We ourselves*
> *stand in the need of being evangelized.* We ourselves
> need to know and meet Christ as He works in the
> world through the power of His Spirit. And it is to this
> world, our world, that we are sent. Its needs and aspi-
> rations are an appeal to the gospel which it is our mis-
> sion to proclaim. (#23) (Italics mine.)

In other words, in our societies that call themselves Christian,
the injustice, oppression, and violence are evidences that the
gospels have not been inculturated into our way of life, our institutions and culture. The gospel remains marginal to the institutions which dominate our lives. The effort to correct this,
the "promotion of justice" as it is called, is seen as a challenge to
breathe the spirit of the gospels into these institutions so that
men and women can live within them and reach the fulfillment
of Christian life. The promotion of justice was seen as an essential aspect of the "service of the Faith." In this, it echoed the emphatic statements of the Synod of Bishops Second General Assembly, "Justice in the World" (1871).

> In the traditionally Christian countries, the
> works we established, the movements we fostered,
> the institutions — retreat houses, schools, univer-
> sities — we set up, continue to render the service of
> faith. But there are many in these countries who can
> no longer be reached by the ministries exercised
> through these works and institutions. The so-called
> Christian countries have themselves become "mis-
> sion" countries. (24b)

Inculturation in the Christian world is defined as the need
to achieve a condition of justice among peoples suffering from
injustice: ". . . it will not be possible to bring Christ to men (and
women) or to proclaim his gospel effectively unless a firm decision is taken to devote ourselves to the promotion of justice." (27)
This reflects the spirit of Vatican II, and the Synod of Bishops',
"Justice in the World," but it acknowledges that the gospel has
not yet been inculturated in many of the nations we now call

Christian. More systematically this is described as "structural
injustice," namely, political and economic institutions structured in such a way that they provide abundance to the affluent
at the expense of the poor. ". . . To work for transformation of
these structures according to the gospel is to work for the
spiritual as well as the material liberation of man, and thus is
intimately related to the work of evangelization." (40)

The Decree makes a brief reference to various cultures in the
world, Christian, non-Christian, and post-Christian. It acknowledges the effort of the Church to bring the gospel to all the
nations of the world, but to respect the differences among them:
". . . she tries today to respect the self-identity of peoples, their
determination to develop their economy and their society, as
well as their understanding of the Christian mystery conform-
able to their history and tradition." (53)

There is a separate Decree #5, devoted to the question of inculturation. It makes special note of the non-Christian worlds of
Asia and Africa. It calls for a special letter of Father General to
the whole Society of Jesus and a more detailed examination of
the issue.

The General of the Jesuits, Father Arrupe, responded to the
request of Decree #5 by a letter devoted to the issue of inculturation. It reflects the spirit of the 32nd General Congregation in
that it sees the need for inculturation as universal:[12]

> Until a few years ago one might have thought it
> was a concern only of countries and continents that
> were different from those in which the gospel was as-
> sumed to have been inculturated for centuries. But
> the galloping pace of change in these latter areas —
> and change has already become a permanent situa-
> tion — persuades us that today there is need of a new
> and continuous inculturation of the faith everywhere
> if we want the gospel to reach modern man and the
> new *sub-cultural groups*. It would be a dangerous
> error to deny that these areas need a re-inculturation
> of the faith. (257)

We must consider ". . . the whole world as one single family,

whose members are beset by the same varied problems." (257)
He reminds Jesuits that, although Ignatius never used the term
"inculturation," its theological content ". . . is present in all his
writings, including the Constitutions." "He keeps insisting that
attention be paid to the circumstances of country, place, different mentalities, and personal temperaments." He quotes Ignatius: "Let them clearly adopt, as far as the Institute of the Society allows, the customs of those peoples (to whom they proclaim the gospel)" and Arrupe adds: that Ignatius ". . . orders
that penances be given to those who do not learn the local language." (259) He asks all Jesuits to search for the "semina verbi"
(seeds of God's word) . . . predestined by Providence for the
building up of truth." (261) These are the characteristics of any
culture which are particularly responsive to the influence of the
gospel.

Arrupe lists the qualities which must be present in anyone
who faces the challenge of inculturation: a unifying vision of salvation history, careful discernment to penetrate to the deepest
meanings of the particular culture; an objectivity and interior
humility which seek to transcend the grievances that persons
may harbor because of previous mistreatment or injustice; per-
severing patience in order to avoid sterile polemics or "easy bar-
gains with error"; a sense of identity with the Church, thinking
with the Church, and *in the Church;* a trust in God's Providence
which protects us from timidity or fear, and from too great reliance on human wisdom.

He sees the great enrichment that inculturation can bring to
the Church, a release from class prejudice and narrow loyalties,
from cultural and racial discrimination. He cautions all not to
allow the effort at inculturation to turn into a hidebound
nationalism or regionalism, diversities which might damage the
bonds of charity. The universalism of the Church must never be
compromised.

The Jesuit Working Paper

One immediate result of the Letter of Pedro Arrupe was a
"working paper" on inculturation that was published in the *Acta*

Romana Societatis Jesus, 1978, together with the Letter.[13] It is
not intended as a statement of policy, but rather a collection of
reflections on the theme, "together with some questions that
may be helpful in seeking solutions to some problems." The reflections are a remarkable statement of the many aspects of inculturation, probably as good an outline as is available for the
study of the issue. It would be of some value to reprint the working paper. It elaborates many of the points of the 32nd general
Congregation and the Letter of Father Arrupe. A brief review of
some of its more significant statements will indicate its importance.

The paper locates itself within the context of the revelation
to Peter and within the context of the current discussion. "God
wants everyone to be saved and attain to knowledge of the truth.
But this must be done within the actual situation of each person;
in other words, within each one's culture." (266) It points to a
major difficulty, not always mentioned in the discussions on inculturation, namely that the gospel has often been presented to
people in such a way that they felt they would become alienated
from their own culture if they accepted it. A number of developments are mentioned as contributing to the current awareness
of the significance of culture: the understanding of culture
which the social sciences have provided in recent decades, the
appearance in relatively short time of many new nations, "the
increasing awareness of personal identity and culture," the
rivalry between conflicting ideologies, and the advance of
technology.

Important in the paper is the position that inculturation is
necessary, not only for non-Christian cultures, but for the many
peoples of the Christian world where modern evils still persist,
and also for what Pedro Arrupe called the sub-cultures of
societies, social classes, for example, or particular groups such
as members of the scientific world who require a presentation of
the gospel in a language and concepts that are meaningful in
their perception of the world. The paper has some strong statements about the need for insight into the life and thinking of the
poor and oppressed. Inculturation may well be a process of a
struggle for justice or liberation. (273)

The paper has a series of "theological reflections." 1) The Incarnation is the motivation and pattern for inculturation. "Just like Him, and because He did so, the Church will become incarnate as vitally and intimately as it can in every culture, being enriched with its values and offering it the unique redemption of Christ, his message, and the resources for a new life." 2) Inculturation is not to be achieved through any diminution of the content of revelation. Every culture, "to be taken up in Christ must share in his death and resurrection, thereby becoming purified, transformed, and perfected by the faith." 3) The analogy of the Trinity is used to express the unity in diversity of a Church in many cultures, the "mutual giving and receiving of one in the other . . . only in giving does one possess, and only in losing can one find." The paper is sensitive to the problem of dependency that is often raised when the Church speaks of bringing the Faith to others. The analogy of the Trinity, the mutual giving and receiving, is used to express an experience of receiving which does not imply dependency. 4) The local Church "must live and express itself in terms of the culture and traditions of that particular people, and in its own language; and 5) "Each local church enriches the others with its own special gifts and in turn is enriched by the others' contribution and by its own share in reflecting a unity which is multiform."

The paper raises the basic question: granted that the Church must never be identified with a particular culture, but is capable of being expressed in the variety of cultures in the world, how does one determine what is "specifically Christian" and what is a "cultural expression of faith" in any particular culture. This is the question that troubled the Apostles; it is the basic question that remains with the Church today. "God does not have favorites, but that anybody of any nationality (culture) who fears God and does what is right is acceptable to him," was the statement of Peter in his brief catechesis to the household of Cornelius (Acts 10). The working paper does not provide any guidelines; it simply states the question as an abiding problem in the process of inculturation. It indicates that, in a constantly changing world, Christians must be prepared to identify the things that constitute a cultural expression and the things which are the essential features of the Faith.

> Christ does not change with the changing times. But the explicit statement of his message does change; and so does the concrete way in which his disciples express their commitment. In the midst of these changes it must always be the Spirit who *renews all things.* (271)

The paper reminds us that the Church has had a variety of cultural expressions in the past; this is the evidence that cultural adaptation can and must be a continuing feature of the Church's life.

The working paper presents a brief statement about the "process of inculturation," especially on the part of Western European Christianity:

> Inculturation presupposes, in the first place, a new mental attitude in the Churches of the old world, both Latin and Oriental: the renunciation of a superiority complex and a monopoly of formal structures. For more than a century now the world has ceased to be markedly European (let alone Mediterranean). And it is fast losing its predominantly western character. . . . The distinction of hemispheres is no longer East and West, but North and South. (273)

The memory of past oppression may prompt new nations to over-react, and "absolutize their own cultural values and shut themselves off from outside influence." (274) This would create serious difficulties for inculturation. "Profound and thoroughgoing interdisciplinary studies will be necessary to know a culture." Men and women born and brought up in a culture can be most helpful. "What must never be done is simply to *play* at inculturation. . . . The alteration of reflection and experience will mark the right rhythm for inculturation."

The paper concludes with the difficulties and tensions, most of which have been noted in the documents reviewed above: the danger of mental inertia, either the superiority complex that sees everything fine as it is with little insight into the contribution that other cultures could make to Christianity, or sees them in need of radical purification; or the opposite danger of regarding any inculturation as impossible; it would be a threat to the purity of Church doctrine. Lack of deep involvement in the concrete details of the lives of people of other cultures, a "laboratory inculturation" as it is called, is also seen as a danger, as well as a liberal mindedness for which anything goes and that fails to make the demands on other cultures which the gospels require. The dialectic tensions are listed below:

— between the universal/immutable and the contingent;

— between the desire to maintain identity (in the Church as well as in a culture) and the need for purification;

— between unity and pluralism;

— between centralization of authority and the principle of subsidiarity;

— between enlightened paternalism and equality of rights;

— between boldness/urgency and prudence. (275)

The paper concludes with some recommendations for the preparation of Jesuits for inculturation. It also has a brief working bibliography.

The Church and the Non-Christian World

The question of inculturation of the Faith in the non-Christian world continues to be an issue of serious and widespread discussion at many levels, some of them official, some of them among theologians and social scientists, some of them on the applied level of pastoral ministry. In the bibliographic note, some of the main sources of these discussions are listed with an annotation about their importance. In this chapter, some of them will be reviewed briefly in order to give the readers a general idea of the nature of the discussions and point them to sources for further study.

One of the boldest statements on a theological level was an address of Karl Rahner on April 8, 1979 at an academic convocation at the Weston School of Theology, Cambridge, Massachusetts. The English translation has been published in *Theological Studies*.[14] In attempting a fundamental theological interpretation of Vatican II, Rahner sees its most important theological significance as "the Church's first official self-actualization as a world Church." (717) Rahner sees three decisively distinct theological periods in the history of the Church: 1) the early and brief period of the Jewish Christians in and around Palestine; 2) the break-through to the Church of the Gentiles, the omission of circumcision, the Mosaic Law, the Hebrew tradition in the development of an authentically Gentile Church. This was a *caesura* (as Rahner calls it) of momentous importance, the opening of the Church to a radically new way of thinking and acting that was to expand into Western Christianity. The history of that event is given in some detail above in Chapter 1. 3) the world church of today, another break-through analogous to that of the break from Jewish Christianity to the Gentile church.

Rahner sees some antecedents of this in the presence for the first time of a notable number of native bishops, constituting a world episcopate, joining with the Pope as the decision-making body of the Church. The *Declaration on the Relation of the Church to non-Christian Religions,* Rahner sees as a "truly positive evaluation of the great world religions initiated for the first time in the doctrinal history of the Church"; (720) and the *Declaration on Religious Liberty* is seen as equally important since the Church "expressly renounced all instruments of force for the proclamation of its faith which do not lie in the power of the gospel itself." (720) Finally in the *Pastoral Constitution on the Church in the Modern World (Gaudium et Spes),* "The Church as a totality becomes conscious of its responsibility for the dawning history of humanity . . . the Third World is truly present as part of the Church and as object of its responsibility."

Rahner raises a question, not always mentioned in discussions of inculturation, about the rapid and radical social and cultural changes occurring in many parts of the Third World. When the question of inculturation is raised, the further question must also be raised: inculturation into what? Into a culture that is disappearing, or an emerging culture, the characteristics of which are still only vaguely seen? Rahner is more explicit than most theologians in stating the specific problems that inculturation will involve:

> . . . Will the new Code of Canon Law . . . avoid the danger of being once again a Western Code that is imposed on the world Church in Latin America, Asia, and Africa? Do not the Roman Congregations still have the mentality of a centralized bureaucracy which thinks it knows best what serves the kingdom of God and the salvation of souls throughout the world and in such decisions takes the mentality of Rome or Italy in a frighteningly naive way as a self-evident standard? Must the marital morality of the Masais in East Africa simply reproduce the morality of Western Christianity, or could a chieftan there, even if he is a Christian, live in the style of the Patriarch Abraham? Must the Eucharist even in Alaska be celebrated with grape wine? (717-18)

All of this is dimly envisaged, as Rahner sees it. But, despite the hesitations and fears, he sees Vatican II as the first official acknowledgement of the Church, not as a Church of Western Europe, but a Church of the world.

Inculturation in Non-Semitic Asia
The Month, March, 1986, 83-87.[15]

An equally perceptive analysis with particular attention to Asia is found in the writings of Father Aloysius Pieris, S.J. He suggests a reflection that so many others have exprerienced:

"What if Saint Paul had founded a Church in Benares, Bangkok, or Beijing, and had he written an epistle to the Christians there . . ." would that have given us an apostolic tradition to follow as the Church seeks to ". . . forge an ecclesial identity in the non-Semitic cultures of Asia?" Pieris does not find any models in the history of the Church that could provide some guidelines for the present challenge. He sees the Latin model as the "incarnation of the Church in a non-Christian culture," and the Greek model as the "assimilation of a non-Christian philosophy." The North European Model he describes as "accommodation to a non-Christian religiosity." He finds none of these applicable to the relationship of the Church to the non-Semitic cultures of Asia. Pieris gives a number of reasons for saying this: The early Fathers had a negative attitude toward the non-Christian religions; they felt that only the *culture* of Rome and the *philosophy* of the Greeks were worth being assumed by the Church. More serious is his conviction that the concept of inculturation conveys a separation of religion and culture which makes no sense to the Asians. The idea of ". . . the insertion of 'the Christian religion minus European culture' into an Asian culture minus non-Christian religion". . . is inconceivable in the South Asian context. . . . What seems possible and even necessary there, is not just inculturation but interreligionisation." (83)

Pieris defines these earlier models of inculturation as "instrumental" — a tendency to select out of an alien religion or culture those elements which could be of service to the Christian religion. This results in what he calls a form of theological vandalism, the appropriation of aspects or symbols of an alien religion which can be adapted to the Christian faith. He sees this as a subtle form of imperialism and refers to the indignation of Buddhists in Thailand because the Church was usurping their sacred symbols for Christian use. (84) He cautions against the danger of inculturation appearing to Asians as a kind of opportunism, namely a declining colonial Christianity seeking to survive by usurping elements of the religions which flourish in Asia. ". . .The inculturation fever might appear to be a desperate last-moment bid to give an Asian facade to a Church which

fails to strike roots in Asian soil because no one dares to break
the Graeco-Roman pot in which it has been existing for four centuries like a stunted *bonsai.*" (84)

Pieris finds a useful analogy in the North European Model of
Christianization, the "accomodation of the Church to a non-
Christian religiosity." The *clannic* societies of the early middle
ages can be compared to the *tribal* societies that survive in Asia.
These are basically religious cultures whose religiousness is essentially *cosmic* ". . . a word we deliberately substitute for the
'animist' of anthropologists."

> It is contrasted with the *metacosmic* religions
> which postulate the existence of a Transphenomenal
> Reality immanently operative in the cosmos and
> soteriologically available within the human person
> either through *agape* (redeeming love) or through
> *gnosis* (redeeming knowledge). Such would be the
> Judaeo-Christian Faiths which are agapeic, and the
> monastic forms of Hinduism, Buddhism, and Taoism
> which are gnostic. (84)

Pieris sees the possibility of a relationship between the two
which would be complementary, neither one replacing the
other, but completing one another ". . . in such a way as to form
a bidimensional soteriology which maintains a healthy tension
between the cosmic *Now,* and the metacosmic *Beyond.*" In this
way Pieris urges the Western Church to ". . . think of inculturation not as an ecclesiastical expansion into non-Christian cultures, but as the forging of an indigenous ecclesiastical identity
from within the soteriological perspectives of the Asian religions." (85) Pieris attributes much of the success of the Church
in Northern Europe to the monks. It was in the formative centuries of Christian monasticism that the "gnostic spirituality of
the non-Christian gradually filtered into the agapeic religiosity
of the monks. . . . If the Western Patriarchate can learn from
its monks to blend the gnostic and the agapeic idioms, it would
know how to appreciate the kind of "inculturation" Asia needs
today.

Pieris then looks to the social realities of Asia's teeming poor

populations and places the "Faith and Justice" concept in a decidedly Asian context. One characteristic of western monasticism was the realization that their asceticism had to be com-
plemented ". . . by an (agapeic) *involvement with the world's
poor* who mediate Christ's presence for us. Thus true Christian
renunciation of wealth was always considered to be made in
favor of the poor so that from the anchoretic inceptions of the
movement . . . the monk's search for God was inseparably associated with their service to and solidarity with the poor. . . "
"When a follower of Jesus opts to be poor for the sake of the gospel, he or she would live not only in solidarity with the Asian
monks in their quest for the *Metacosmic* Reality, but more so in
solidarity with the Asian Poor who aspire for a *cosmic* order that
is more just and holy." (86) "The monastic instinct of the Church,
if sharpened by the gospel and not blunted by political naivete,
cannot go wrong in Asia." Thus Pieris links together the Asian
concept of liberation from the world, and the Western concept of
liberation from injustice as elements involved in effective "inculturation."

Pieris has perceived the implications of inculturation in a
much sharper way than is evident in the documents of the
Church. He sees the need of a *caesura,* as Rahner describes it,
between the absorption of the Faith in Western European culture and the implications of its inculturation in the profoundly
religious cultures of Asia, where the religion is the culture and
the culture is the religion. Yet he is not fearful that the essence
of Christianity would be lost in the process; it would find a rich
fulfillment as a metacosmic reality, complementing the cosmic
reality of the cultures of Asia.

Pieris has written widely on the theme summarized above.
His writing constitutes one significant aspect of the dialogue
that seeks to appreciate the full meaning of the non-Christian
cultures and the implications for them and for the Christian
world of a process of inculturation.

Inculturation in Africa

Nowhere is the issue of inculturation more actively discussed than in Africa. An abundant literature has developed

about Africa in recent years. It is summarized and briefly analyzed in an excellent article by Justin S. Ukpong,[16] of the Catholic Institute of West Africa at Port Harcourt, Nigeria. Ukpong makes it clear that inculturation in Africa is a different problem than inculturation in Asia. "Though certain themes in Asian culture are similar to those found in African culture, e.g., the sense of community, wholeness of life, and an integrated view of reality, there are significant differences in the religious contexts of the two continents and the people's world view within which theology is set." (534) Ukpong quotes Pieris that Asian religions have become highly integrated and contextualized in historical religious traditions. There are also distinct philosophies to contend with. Whereas "In Africa, . . . the only other religion is the African traditional religion." (534) Ukpong thinks that this religious tradition has a concept of God that is quite compatible with that of Christians; Africa has also been under the influence of Christian missionaries; and, despite their associations with colonialism, African perceptions of God have been touched by them.

There has been a long history of "inculturation theology" in Africa. "This involves a conscious engagement of European thinking and African religious thought in serious dialogue for the purpose of integrating Christianity into the life and culture of African people." (501) More recently, two other theological trends have become prominent, South African Black Theology and African Liberation Theology, sometimes related to the socio-economic realities of Africa; sometimes a reflection of South American Liberation Theology; sometimes a combination of both.

Ukpong describes the earlier forms of "inculturation theology" as a form of accommodation. This was associated with the missionary activity that was prevalent in Africa since the last century, activity which is reflected in the rapidly growing numbers of Christians in Africa. However,

> In spite of this phenomenal success, the widespread syncretistic life of many African Christians calls into question the extent to which Christianity

has been assimilated and digested by them. . . . A
careful analysis of the situation reveals that the observed acts of syncretism among African Christians
is not so much a sign of lack of Christian commitment
as an expression of the fact that Christianity, as
transmitted to the African, has not been made to respond fully to his culturally based religious aspira-
tions. (510)

Ukpong's analysis of the involvement of culture is clear, simple, and convincing. He acknowledges the influence of the social
sciences in clarifying the concept of culture and its involvement
in every aspect of human life. ". . . Man reflects on divine truths
from a certain cultural standpoint. The fruits of such reflection
formulated as theology necessarily bear the imprint of that culture. Culture must, therefore, be seen as an inseparable part of
any theological system." (511) Ukpong finds the earlier efforts
at inculturation, what he calls the accommodation approach, to
be limited and inadequate. And it results from the deep preoccupation with the need to distinguish "essential Christianity"
from its "cultural expression." This results in a form of "translat-
ing" the Christian message from its Western cultural setting
into an African cultural setting. "This leads (the theologian) to
focus largely on the beliefs and principles of Christianity" and
". . . seems to assume the Western format for theology as nor-
mative." (515) This is the critical issue as Rahner and Pieris
have analyzed it. Ukpong is clear about his assessment:

Its concept of Christianity is based on a theology
of revelation that emphasizes the disclosure of doctrine, hence there is great concern to identify the ker-
nal of the message. With this theology of revelation,
the assumed attitude toward African traditional religion is mistrust; hence the need for rigorous criticism
of elements and themes taken from it for the trans-
mission of its message. (515)

This emphasis on doctrine, Ukpong explains, is not responsive
to the African religious experience. ". . . African traditional

religion is a way of life and not a collection of doctrines. African theology in this approach becomes life-oriented as opposed to a knowledge-oriented theology." A more modern concept of "inculturation" is responsive to this type of experience.

A typical example in the liturgy is the Zaire Mass, whose format is different from the traditional one with the following prominent features. At the beginning of the Mass there is a long litany invoking the ancestors; the penitential rite comes after the homily, followed by aspersion and the kiss of peace; the Eucharistic prayers are composed according to African prayer pattern; there is much interpolation, singing, dancing, drumming, and bodily gesture throughout the Mass. (516)

This is a departure from the format of Western theology. Ukpong describes it as a result of two significant factors, (1) "a return to the original sources of Christian expression, i.e., the Bible and tradition;" and (2) "a total opening out to the whole of African traditional religion and culture as opposed to a mere selection of themes from them." (516)

The task basically involves confronting the Christian faith and African culture so that faith enlightens culture, and in the process there results the interpenetration and integration of both. The basic data of revelation as contained in Scripture and tradition are critically reflected upon for the purpose of giving them African cultural expression. From this is born a new theological reflection that is African and Christian. (516)

This presents the issue very sharply. It suggests a return to scripture and tradition as the sources of Christian life, to be given expression in the full experience of African religious life. But it by-passes the structure of Western Christianity, rooted in Greek philosophy and Roman culture. Just as the Gentile Church represented a complete break from the Hebrew religious tradition, and flowered in a process of reflection on the scriptures and the Apostolic tradition, Ukpong sees the possibility of an African Christianity flowering the the same way.

Ukpong then reviews briefly the works of major scholars and writers engaged in the discussion of inculturation of Christianity in Africa, and gives a brief critique of each of them. In general, he finds serious limitations in most of the African theologies because "they do not make explicit those metaphysical, epistemological, and anthropological assumptions that lie behind these theories." (520) "Finally, Catholic authors in particular must be reminded of the need to have their works grounded on a solid biblical foundation." And he concludes:

> Already there exists a gap between the people's way of life and some of the Christian principles they have been taught. This has been mainly because Christianity has been presented to them as a set of principles and not as a way of life; for, to become a way of life for Africans, Christianity must be made relevant to and expressive of the way they live and think. (520)

Black Theology has developed in Africa mainly in South Africa, under the influence of American Blacks, since the experience of Blacks in South Africa is similar to the experience of Blacks in the United States. Black Theology sees the gospel message as one of liberation. It is critical of the failure among those who call themselves Christians to follow the gospel of love and justice which Jesus preached. Ukpong sees Black Theology as a regional movement that does not offer the promise of a widespread African response. Liberation Theology, related to the oppression and injustice which exist in many parts of Africa, will enjoy a more widespread response. "By posing the issue of color and poverty for theological answers, black theology and liberation theology point to the fact that theology should constantly seek out human problems and give relevant answers to them whenever and wherever they exist." (536)

The Church and the Emerging World

The three authors, Rahner, Pieris, and Ukpong all focus on

the problem of the need of the Church to break out of the confining limits of Western Christian theology to open the Church to inculturation in ways of life in which Western perceptions are not meaningful. Religion is the totality of life for the Asians, as Pieris explains it; African traditional religion is a way of life, not a collection of doctrines, as Ukpong explains it. And Rahner asks whether the Church can break out of Western structures and be willing to be inculturated in worlds where religious experience is strikingly different.

Ukpong thinks that "accommodation" theology was too much preoccupied with identifying the essence of Christianity from its cultural expression. But this is fundamentally the issue.

It is not my purpose here to attempt a critique of any of the authors I summarized. My objective was to give a brief presentation of the issue and the way the Church has responded in official statements; the way others such as the Jesuits have been responding; and the problem as presented by some of the more advanced thinkers and scholars. Like the Apostles at the First Council of Jerusalem (*Acts 15*), we face the challenge with a clear understanding of the issues. Its solution will require much more than workshops in intercultural communication, although these will be essential, especially for people who are involved in face-to-face contact with persons of different forms of religious belief and practice.

The response to the Hispanic presence in the United States is much easier to deal with than inculturation in Asia or Africa. Here the challenge can be met by continued preparation of Catholics to understand the Hispanic culture and the way to receive them into the life of the Church in the United States. They come from a Catholic world with a Catholic tradition of its own. Whether a continuing process of cultural pluralism is possible, or some kind of assimilation, this kind of adjustment is comparatively simple.

More difficult is the inculturation of the faith into the dominant culture of the United States. This also is an experience

within a basic framework of Christian values. The officially
stated values and ideals of the nation are respectful of the Christian values that have guided Western Christianity. However,
the modern trend toward secularism, a dominant consumerism,
a preoccupation with the interests of national defense and security at the expense of the service of the people, the problem of
justice in relation to the large numbers of the poor, these are
some of the features of American life which constitute a challenge to the faith in American culture.

Finally, the larger issue of inculturation involves the opening of the Church to the non-Christian world, particularly Africa
and Asia. It is here that the really profound difficulties arise
about the relation of the Church to very different religious traditions. The preoccupation of the Church with the "essence" of
Christianity cannot be brushed aside. Jesus did call Himself
"The Truth" as well as "The Way" and "The Life." His question
to the Apostles was direct: "Who do you say that I am?" The answer had a cognitive dimension. Missioners and theologians and
Church authorities will struggle with this challenge of the opening of the Church to the non-Christian world. It will not be without pain similar to that of the early Christians. But we can trust
that the Spirit will guide the Church in the twenty-first century
as He guided it in the first.

Notes

1. The Pastoral Constitution on the Church in the Modern World (*Gaudium
et Spes*) Part 2, Chapter 2, "The Proper Development of Culture," in *The Documents of Vatican II*, edited by Walter M. Abbott, S.J. (New York: Herder and
Herder, 1966).

The most important official statement on inculturation is found in the apostolic exhortation of Pope Paul VI, *Evangelii Nuntiandi (Evangelization in the
Modern World)* December 8, 1975. AAS 68 (1/31/76), 5-76. The English translation is published in *The Pope Speaks*, V. 21, n. 1 (1976) 4-51. This has extensive
documentation. This was followed by a statement from the IV Synod of Bishops,
(1977), *Message to the People of God, Origins* V. 7, n. 21 (Nov. 10, 1977), 321 ff.
Other literature will be noted in the course of this chapter. The standard reference source is found in *Bibliografia Missionaria,* published by the German Oblate Fathers at the Pontifical Mission Library, Piazza di Spagna, 48, Rome,
Italy.

2. The Declaration of the Synod, *Evangelization of the Modern World,* is found in *The Gospel of Peace and Justice,* ed. Joseph Gremillion, (Maryknoll, New York: Orbis Press, 1976), p. 594.

3. Bernardino de Sahagun, *General History of the Things of New Spain,* (Florentine Codex) Tr. by Arthur J.O. Anderson and Charles E. Dibble, 12 volumes, 13 parts. (Santa Fe: New Mexico School of American Research and the University of Utah, 1950). These are the remarkable studies of Sahagun, fortunately retrieved from obscurity, the most reliable source of information about the religious beliefs and practices of the Aztecs.

4. Latin American Episcopal Conference, (CELAM) *The Church In the Present Day Transformation of Latin America.* . . ., Vol. I, p. 9.

5. *Ibid.,* p. 41.

6. Address of Paul VI to the Peasants, Mosquera, Colombia, August 23, 1968, quoted in Latin American Episcopal Conference, *ibid.,* Vol. 2, p. 213.

7. Latin American Episcopal Conference, *ibid.,* p. 216.

8. *Justice in the World,* Synod of Bishops, Second General Assembly (November 30, 1971) reprinted in J. Gremillion (ed.), *The Gospel of Peace and Justice,* (Maryknoll, NY: Orbis, 1976), 513-29.

9. Society of Jesus, *Documents of the Thirty-First General Congregation,* (1965-66) and *Documents of the Thirty-Second General Congregation,* 1974-75. The Institute of Jesuit Sources, 3700 West Pine Boulevard, Saint Louis, Missouri, 63108.

10. *Acta Romana: Societatis Iesu,* 711, 1949, page 714.

11. 31st General Congregation, The Institute of Jesuit Sources, St. Louis: Missouri, 1977, Nos. 569-579.

12. Pedro Arrupe, S.J., "On Inculturation: A Letter to the Whole Society of Jesus," *Acta Romana Societatis Jesu,* Rome, Curia Praepositi Generalis, 1979), Vol. XVIII, N. 2, p. 257 (pages noted in quotes).

13. *Ibid.,* pp. 266-81.

14. Karl Rahner: "Towards a Fundamental Theological Interpretaion of Vatican II," *Theological Studies* 40 (December, 1979), 716-27.

15. Aloysious Pieris, S.J., "Inculturation in Non-Semitic Asia," *The Month* (March, 1986), 83-87.

16. Justin Upkong, "The Emergence of African Theologies," *Theological Studies* 45 (1984), 501-36.